Praise for *Alone in Antarctica*:

'Felicity's dynamic and inspiring storytelling links us all to our own crossing, helping us all push beyond our fears to reach our goals. Her descriptions of the ice and her honesty of the feelings it brings forth, stir our love for that magnificent place and the lifestyle of the challenge – we want to return!'

Ann Bancroft and Liv Arnesen, polar explorers

'Felicity's gripping adventure captures the thrill and fear of Antarctic exploration'   Ranulph Fiennes

'Resilient, brave, daring, foolhardy, admirable and hugely likeable'
Joanna Lumley

Praise for *Call of the White*:

'An uplifting and enthralling feat; I take my fur hat off to all those who answered this call of the white. An inspiring tale which will stir the hearts of women and men around the world'

Benedict Allen

'A unique expedition... this story is true inspiration to venture beyond your comfort zone'   *Wanderlust* magazine

'Enthralling'   *Woman's Weekly*

'Uplifting'   *Adventure Travel* magazine

ALONE IN ANTARCTICA

Copyright © Felicity Aston, 2013

Photographs © Felicity Aston

All rights reserved.

No part of this book may be reproduced by any means, nor transmitted, nor translated into a machine language, without the written permission of the publishers.

Felicity Aston has asserted her right to be identified as the author of this work in accordance with sections 77 and 78 of the Copyright, Designs and Patents Act 1988.

Condition of Sale
This book is sold subject to the condition that it shall not, by way of trade or otherwise, be lent, resold, hired out or otherwise circulated in any form of binding or cover other than that in which it is published and without a similar condition including this condition being imposed on the subsequent purchaser.

Summersdale Publishers Ltd
46 West Street
Chichester
West Sussex
PO19 1RP
UK

www.summersdale.com

Printed and bound by CPI Group (UK) Ltd, Croydon, CR0 4YY

ISBN: 978-1-84953-432-1

Substantial discounts on bulk quantities of Summersdale books are available to corporations, professional associations and other organisations. For details contact general enquiries: telephone: +44 (0) 1243 771107 or email: enquiries@summersdale.com.

ALONE
IN ANTARCTICA

WITH A FOREWORD BY JOANNA LUMLEY

FELICITY ASTON

summersdale

CONTENTS

CONTENTS

FOREWORD

BY JOANNA LUMLEY

I met Felicity Aston at the Royal Geographical Society: we were speaking about journeys we had made, along with Robin Knox-Johnston and Ranulph Fiennes, so I was pretty comprehensively out of my depth, as all I was going to talk about was being on a desert island for nine days, visited every day by a small film crew. This could hardly be on the same page as Felicity's phenomenal journey, so I was especially touched when she asked me to write the foreword to this book. What had struck a chord with her apparently was how we both, as women, had experienced sensations of utter alone-ness, cartwheeling minds, mild hallucinations and a feeling that nature, for want of a better word, was watching out for us. It is always fascinating to hear how others have coped with hardships with which we in some way feel we can empathise. I started reading the book at once, as soon as she sent it to me: I read it straight through and now try to herd my stunned impressions into some kind of shape.

'Alone' usually means without anyone else: 'I'll come alone', 'I was alone on the beach', 'Leave me alone'. When we use the word we imagine that, although the writer is without human company, evidence of humanity is around: houses, books, roads, fields, footprints of human existence. But imagine 'alone' meaning to be without the world as we know it, without horizons or daylight, without distance or objects to focus on, without high or low, when all perspective is lost; and then try to think of that weird and dreadful condition day after day (if you can tell the difference between day and night) combined with danger, complete isolation, when your physical toughness is tested to the extreme and your mind begins to somersault off towards the edges of sanity... This is the 'alone' that Felicity Aston chose to face in her astonishing journey across Antarctica.

And 'cold' – what does cold mean to you? Putting on gloves and a thick coat, jumping up and down, sitting on the radiator...? It doesn't usually mean having icicles on your eyelashes, your bra filled with batteries and lighters, being locked inside layers of frozen clothing.

Crying your eyes out, knowing no one is coming to help you as you are miles from any possible sign of life, surrounded by the most hostile conditions on Earth, is not an everyday event in our normal lives, and this is the point: nor is it normal in hers. Resilient, brave, daring, foolhardy, admirable and hugely likeable, she traces for us the whole journey and why she made it in the first place: her terrors and routines, her eating habits (gnawing half-frozen food and posting tiny bits of chocolate through her breathing aperture) and dream-like encounters with the sun, her guardian and her inspiring companion.

Her writing is so modest and humble that it is sometimes hard to grasp the scale of her record-breaking adventure. What comes over strongly is her sheer perseverance, her dogged determination.

> *If you can force your heart and nerve and sinew*
> *To serve your turn long after they are gone,*
> *And so hold on when there is nothing in you*
> *Except the will that says to them: 'Hold on!'*

Felicity's version of Kipling's words is simply: 'Keep getting out of the tent.' Her greatest fear, it turns out, is the fear of being alone: and when she decides that she need never be completely alone again, ever, for the rest of her life, it seems like a sign for us all. Once you have faced your demons down and clung on to the bitter end, terror melts away in the warmth of the sun, who is, after all, your friend.

PROLOGUE

ALONE

The plane had become a tiny black blob in the pale sky. I could still hear the distinctive drone of its engines but with every breath the sound became fainter. I closed my eyes to focus my ears on the noise but it was slowly, and inevitably, blotted out by the silence. When I opened my eyes again, the plane had gone.

I was alone.

I stood motionless for a second, breathing in the cold air. Even the smallest of movements sounded brutally intrusive in the stillness: the rasp of brittle fabrics, the polystyrene squeak of my boots in the snow. I turned on the spot, running my gaze slowly over the horizon, trying to take in my surroundings. After months of contemplating this place on the map it seemed unreal that I was now physically here. To my right was the flat expanse of the Ross Ice Shelf, a featureless divide of white snow and blue sky, while to my left were the Transantarctic Mountains which extended in an unbroken line as far as I could see in either direction. The sun, still high in the sky although it was almost midnight, bounced from the mountainsides of vibrant orange rock and turquoise ice. Each peak appeared intimately close-by even though I knew that I could travel for hours towards them and still not touch stone.

As I looked in wonder at all this surreal magnificence one thought echoed through my brain: in all this landscape, in all this space, I was the only living thing. I could search every fold of rock, every block of ice and not find so much as a nesting bird, a minute fly or a single blade of hardy grass. Even bacteria have a hard time surviving in this part of the world. The nearest open water where any wildlife was to be found was more than 700 kilometres away to the north and the nearest human habitation perhaps as much as 1,000 kilometres to the west. The scale of the emptiness was almost too much to absorb. I dragged my attention away from the distant horizon and refocused.

'Time to get sorted,' I told the air.

Moving purposefully towards the two small plastic sledges at my feet, each containing a bag that bulged with food, stove fuel and equipment, I pulled open the zip of the bag nearest to me. As I sifted through the contents I realised I had forgotten what I was looking for.

'Tent first, idiot,' I reminded myself.

I heaved the neatly rolled tent from the second sledge but as I did so several precious items of equipment spilled out onto the snow – an amateur mistake. I scooped them up anxiously before any unexpected breeze could scatter my vital belongings. Moving too quickly, I stumbled in the snow over my own feet and fell heavily onto my sledge.

'What is wrong with me?' I asked aloud in angry frustration.

I looked down at my hands which were visibly trembling. My chest felt constricted, making it difficult to breathe, and my heart was running so fast that I could hear the thump of blood in my ears as clear as a drumbeat. An itch of adrenalin crawled along my arms to each fingertip and made the muscles in my legs quiver. My eyes rested on the mountains snaking off into the distance and I was struck with sudden understanding. I knew exactly what was wrong with me. This was what it feels like to be terrified. This was a physical response to the horror I felt at being so alone. Every fibre of my body was yelling at me that something was terribly, terribly wrong.

Panic filled my chest like a slow rising bubble threatening to block off the air to my lungs. It burned in my stomach like corrosive acid and I felt choked. It wasn't that I feared for my life or for my safety, it was the alone-ness itself that scared me. I have always been comfortable in my own company and often travel by myself to remote places but this was a whole new level of isolation; to be so far not just from other human beings but from any form of life whatsoever. The sense of absolute loneliness was instant, overwhelming and completely crushing.

Out of nowhere my brain told me what to do. 'Let the fear in,' it ordered and I obeyed. I slumped onto my knees and held my head in my gloved hands. My face contorted, the tears hot in my eyes. At first there was no sound, then I heard a strange strangled sob that scared me with its desperation.

I cried from my soul.

The tears splashed onto the snow by my knees and even in the depths of my turmoil I noticed that they left miniature impressions in the surface as they froze – tiny little tear-prints in the ice.

I'm not sure how long I sat in the snow sobbing but eventually the tears stopped and I stared at the spot in the sky that had swallowed the plane. No matter how hard I cried, that plane wasn't coming back. Already the cold was beginning to make itself felt on my face. I couldn't stay out in the open. I needed to pitch my tent and sort the equipment that was now messily strewn around my sledges. Immediately I felt slightly embarrassed. Ten years of experience in the polar regions had culminated in this, a pitiful weeping fool. I stood up and rolled my tent out in the snow where I would spend the night. My hands still shook, my heart thumped more violently than ever and although I tried hard to concentrate on what I was doing, I couldn't quite shake the image of my tears falling onto the snow, frozen in its white crust.

I had the feeling that this vast, lonely continent would take much more from me before I was done.

CHAPTER ONE

EVERY STEP

The first time I saw Antarctica was from a ship. I was twenty-three and on my way to Rothera Research Station, a British Antarctic Survey base on the Antarctic Peninsula, which would be my place of work and my home for the next two and a half years. The voyage from the Falkland Islands took a fortnight, sailing alongside some of the most spectacular scenery on the planet. The Peninsula seemed to be one continuous line of sharp peaks, their tips barely visible above the swathes of snow and ice that smothered them, while at their feet the ocean was glutinous with the cold and as black as liquorice.

It was a purely geologic landscape; no trees or buildings to give any sense of scale. It was only when Rothera came into view, a tiny cluster of green rectangles clinging to an area of exposed rock on the coastline, that the true enormity of the terrain revealed itself. It became clear that the peaks of the Peninsula that had looked close enough to touch were actually colossal titans tens of kilometres away and what had appeared to be delicate webs of snow criss-crossing the rock faces were in fact immense tracts of ice clinging to the mountainsides in motionless cascades.

From its rocky perch, Rothera looked out across a bay rimmed with mountains where chaotic icefalls filled the spaces between the peaks and covered the ground to the shore. The confusion of fractured ice looked almost frothy, so that the mountains took on the appearance of courtiers wearing fussy cravats and frills of lace.

Over the next twenty-eight months I spent a lot of time gazing out from the station at the profile of those mountains and it became as familiar to me as my garden at home. When the weather was relatively warm I'd sit on the veranda outside the base chatting to friends and colleagues as the midnight sun lit the crest of the mountains. Then, as the days darkened into winter and Rothera emptied, I'd often watch through the ice-rimmed window of my office as the sky turned vibrant shades of pink, orange and indigo, staining the snow-covered slopes.

The bay that had been a dark slash of ice-speckled sea when I'd arrived gradually froze until the scenery was one unbroken landscape of white. As the temperatures got colder, tiny wisps of steam rose from myriad cracks in the glaciers that poured into the sea from the flanks of each peak. The steam looked like smoke from unseen campfires, as if there was a hidden community living deep in the fissures.

By midwinter the sun was too weary to rise above the horizon and the only light was a faint cinnamon glow for a few hours a day. Sometimes this was enough to see a reflected glimmer from the snow-encased summits and to be able to trace the line of their backs. When the moon was bright the mountains reappeared as clearly as if the sun had returned. The silver radiance, although not as bright as daylight, seemed to make every detail sharper, like a perfectly exposed black-and-white photograph. Those metallic evenings were the Peninsula at its most beautiful.

I was at the station as one of the meteorologists responsible for monitoring climate and ozone. One of my regular jobs was to measure the accumulation of snow using a grid of snowstakes that had been established a significant distance from the base. Travelling out to the snowstakes on snowmobiles was one of my favourite weekly chores. Usually I took someone with me but a few months after I arrived, I decided to go alone for the first time. It was nearing the end of the summer season and the chill of an oncoming winter was in the air. I coaxed one of the station's elderly snowmobiles into life and stashed my notebooks and records under the seat before setting off. Following a line of flags I motored away from the station buildings, past the aircraft hangar and the outlying depots of fuel drums and sledges, onto the steep local glacier. As my snowmobile ground uphill, the land to my left fell away into ice cliffs, revealing the blinding glint of open water. It stretched off towards the only straight horizon visible from Rothera – that of the sea. Veering right, I followed the flagline beneath a spiky wave of dark rock called Reptile Ridge that towered overhead as it curved inland. After a few kilometres the route opened out onto a large plain. I knew that if I continued around to the left I would come to Vals, a gentle slope on the side of Reptile Ridge that we used for skiing and snowboarding, dragging each other to the top on long ropes towed behind snowmobiles. But today Vals was empty and I was travelling away from the ridge across the open space ahead. My snowmobile was heavy, more metal box than high-performance machine, but with my thumb pressed flat against the throttle I could feel it picking up speed on the flatter ground and I enjoyed the freedom of flying over the snow, letting my eyes drift across the soft curves of the undulating landscape. Solitary peaks rose above the snow surface leaving graceful arcs and semi-circles of blue and purple shadows on the otherwise raw white. Overhead, thin high cloud traced delicate curlicues in the sky as if mimicking the geometry of the shadows on the ground. Taking it all in, my breath caught in my chest and I let my thumb slip off the throttle so that the snowmobile came to a gentle stop. I stood up on the clattering machine and let myself indulge in the euphoria that had welled up inside me. I threw open my arms as if I could extend them around the whole landscape, around the whole of Antarctica. I had the overwhelming urge to scoop it all up, to skim over the flawless surface, to lose myself in its immaculate vastness. I stood there for ages feeling my heart expand to envelop the entire continent. There was nowhere on the planet that could be more fulfilling, nowhere on Earth I would rather be. I had found my perfect place, my perfect match.

In many ways that sense of elation has never left me. Two and a half years later when it was time to leave Antarctica for the first time, I stood out on the ship's deck and watched the skyline I knew so well gradually morph into an unfamiliar view as we sailed out of the bay and into a different perspective. A friend who had worked on the base with me and who was also saying his goodbyes to Antarctica came to stand close by in companionable silence.

'I thought you'd be in tears, Fliss,' he said eventually.

It struck me as odd too that I didn't feel more emotional. I wasn't entirely sure why. Perhaps it was because after such a long time away from home, I was ready to go despite my sadness. Or perhaps it was because a part of me knew that it wouldn't be long before I was back in Antarctica, even though I had no idea at the time how or why I would return. I remember looking into the hard black surface of the Southern Ocean, trying to imagine what my plan would be when I got home. I attempted to picture myself in all sorts of employment but somehow I just couldn't envisage fitting in to any one profession. I assumed that the answer would emerge in time – but it turned out that my inability to see myself with a job was prophetic. To date, my position at Rothera remains the closest I've ever come to having conventional employment. On my return I worked in London briefly, organising expeditions for young people, but I only lasted a matter of months before resigning. I knew instinctively that I didn't belong in an office.

Instead, I began to organise expeditions of my own to the polar regions, putting together interesting teams to go to isolated places, but it was to be six years before I found a way back to Antarctica. In 2009 I trained and led an unconventional team of novice explorers with the aim of skiing together to the South Pole. The eight-woman team was from Brunei Darussalam, Cyprus, Ghana, India, Jamaica, New Zealand, Singapore and the UK. Most of the women had never spent a night in a tent, put on a pair of skis or experienced sub-zero temperatures before joining the expedition. However, despite the physical challenge of the environment and the human challenge of working together as a group, we skied more than 900 kilometres from the coast of Antarctica to the South Pole in thirty-eight days. This was the first time I'd had an opportunity to reach the South Pole and I couldn't have wished for a better way to arrive, at the head of the largest and most international team of women ever to ski to ninety degrees south.

In the hours after arriving at the bottom of the world, I sat in the cramped hospitality tent drinking tea, listening to the rest of the women excitedly announce our success to their families over the satellite phone and feeling myself relax in a way that I hadn't been able to for months. Fatigue gradually overtook each of my team-mates in turn and they drifted off to our tents pitched nearby. I was enjoying the moment too much to submit to sleep just yet so I walked back to the South Pole a few hundred metres away. The spot was marked with a red and white striped pole topped by a glossy silver sphere surrounded by the flags of the original Antarctic Treaty Nations. Apart from the snap of the flags in the wind, all was quiet. I had the end of the Earth to myself.

I stood for a moment gazing at the horizon we had skied over, letting my memory trek backward over the miles we had travelled. The cold burned the exposed skin on my face and made my eyes water, so I turned out of the wind and studied the opposite horizon. My imagination instinctively raced over the kilometres of wind-furrowed snow, creating mental visions of the landscape beyond that I had only seen on maps: an immense empty plateau, then a wall of serried mountains where the ice spilled between the peaks onto the ocean, forming a great floating platform – the Ross Ice Shelf. Absently, I wondered how it would feel to set off towards those mountains. I felt a gentle pull toward that imagined landscape. Tired and aching though I was, I knew with certainty that I could continue beyond the Pole if I had the opportunity – but could I make it all the way to the mountains, and then on as far as the Ross Ice Shelf? Could I ski across the entire continent from one coast to the other – and could I do it alone?

This wasn't a recent idea; the concept had been in my head so long that I couldn't remember exactly where it had first come from.

During the previous thirty-eight days the team had travelled in single file, taking turns to navigate from the front of the line. When it was my turn to lead I'd often pretended that the women behind me had disappeared and that I was out there alone. I'd look around at the white expanse and try to imagine what it would feel like to have that empty landscape to myself, to have no voices around me, no sense of movement apart from my own.

The notion of being alone in Antarctica both thrilled and appalled me. Back at home in the UK I would sometimes dream about it and wake up in my bed shaking with terror at the thought. Even as I reassured myself that it wasn't real and as the relief calmed my fast-beating heart, a part of me knew with some dread that this idea wasn't going away. Now that the proposition of crossing Antarctica by myself had taken hold, my choices were to see it through or to live with regret for the rest of my life. It was bizarre how a plan that caused me so much fear could become such an unshakeable ambition. My instinctive response was to shrink away from the idea and yet I wanted to make this journey with every fibre of my being.

I examined my own motives to try and understand why this journey more than any other had captivated me. Past expeditions had pushed me in a variety of ways: physically, emotionally, as a person and as a leader; but, to date, I didn't feel that I had found my limits. I knew I still had more to give and it seemed that going alone was an obvious way to challenge myself more than I ever had before. There was something about the completeness of crossing the continent, of travelling from one coast to the other, that appealed to me – a chance to see an entire cross-section of this most enigmatic of places. There was beauty in the simplicity of it but, as I was to discover, the details of the plan were anything but simple.

Antarctica is a vaguely circular continent with the South Pole roughly at its centre. Looking at a map it appears that two large bites have been taken out of the landmass; the one at the top is filled with the Ronne Ice Shelf while the one at the bottom, almost directly opposite, is filled with the Ross Ice Shelf. The route between the Ronne Ice Shelf and the South Pole is relatively straightforward. Starting at a point called Hercules Inlet it is a straight line southward for 1,100 kilometres to the South Pole. It is a route that has been followed by dozens of expeditions over the years and was very similar to the one I had skied with the team. Travelling between the South Pole and the Ross Ice Shelf was a little harder. A bit of research quickly showed that very few expeditions ventured this side of the Pole because it was so difficult (and expensive) to get logistical support. I began to refer to it as the 'wrong side' of Antarctica.

The crux of the problem was getting through the Transantarctic Mountains. This chain of peaks forms a wall of rock that curves like an eyebrow over the Ross Ice Shelf and marks out the edge of the continent. Ice from the plateau, moving somewhat like runny icing poured onto the centre of an uneven cake, glides slowly from the elevated interior of Antarctica to its fringes. It pours through any gaps in the barrier of mountains along its edge to form great glaciers that trace sinuous channels to the coast. These glaciers are the only routes through the mountain ranges but they are not easily travelled. The ice of the glaciers is often deeply fissured making them dangerous pathways – particularly if I was to be on my own with nobody to tie myself to, nobody to rescue me and nobody to raise the alarm should I fall into one of the many crevasses.

The largest of the glaciers through the Transantarctic Mountains is the infamous Beardmore. This long, ponderous runway of ice that buckles and fractures for nearly 160 kilometres on the eastern side of the Ross Ice Shelf was used by both Shackleton and Scott during the first exploratory expeditions to Antarctica in the early 1900s. Scott's Norwegian rival, Roald Amundsen, favoured the shorter, steeper (but equally lethal) Axel Heiberg glacier tucked into the top corner of the Ross Ice Shelf, where the distance to the South Pole is shortest. Since then, only a handful of expeditions have followed these pioneering routes and even fewer have attempted new ones. In the 1950s Sir Edmund Hillary led a convoy of modified farm tractors up the Skelton Glacier, close to the Beardmore, as part of Sir Vivian Fuchs's mechanised crossing of Antarctica and, more recently, Ann Bancroft and Liv Arnesen made a descent of the Shackleton Glacier in 2000.

Blazing my own trail along an unknown glacier – alone in one of the remotest parts of Antarctica – was not an option. I didn't have the skill, confidence or appetite for that level of danger. Instead, I considered each of the known routes in turn. The Beardmore and Skelton glaciers were both on the western side of the Ross Ice Shelf and would add considerable distance to my journey, so I focused on the glaciers on the eastern side of the ice shelf, the Shackleton and the Axel Heiberg.

Norwegian explorer, Borge Ousland, had chosen to descend the Axel Heiberg during his solo transantarctic expedition in 1997. His book gave a lot of detail about the route down the glacier and had plenty of terrifying pictures of fractured ice and partially concealed cracks of monstrous proportions. The top of the glacier was known as the 'Devil's Dancefloor' because of the sheer number and intricacy of crevasses. The route looked highly complicated and very risky to travel alone. Images of the Axel Heiberg filtered into my dreams, filling them with lurid visions of a long, lonely death at the bottom of a cold crevasse.

The Shackleton was little better. In an account of their traverse of the glacier in 2000, Liv Arnesen and Ann Bancroft describe a nightmare terrain of crevasses concealed by rotten ice. Repeatedly they fell through the surface, usually getting wedged thigh-deep but occasionally ending up dangling by their elbows over cavernous spaces.

'We would later name this place Hell,' records Ann.

Liv had a particularly close escape, finding herself staring down into a blue-black abyss, saved only by some webbing around her wrist that had snagged on a lump of ice. It allowed her just enough time to gain some purchase on the wall of the crevasse and lift herself out.

'I still have nightmares about what happened on the Shackleton Glacier,' she writes. 'To this day it remains one of the most terrifying experiences I've had in all my travels.'

Reading their recollections left me feeling faintly nauseous. I couldn't justify taking such a risk by myself. It seemed that neither the Shackleton nor the Axel Heiberg was a viable option and without a route through the Transantarctic Mountains, my plans stalled – but the ambition continued to stalk my daydreams.

Antarctica was never far from my mind, even as I turned my attention to other commitments. I regularly give talks across the UK and further afield in Europe and America, sharing stories and lessons learnt from past adventures. Audiences can vary from a school hall of wide-eyed juniors keen to learn about avoiding polar bears in the Arctic to select groups of executives more interested in a fresh look at leadership or successful team dynamics. The variety is something I thrive on, even though travelling from talk to talk can be occasionally chaotic, but I find it a rewarding way to make a living. I enjoy telling a story, be it through writing or speaking, and relish the fact that people from diverse backgrounds and situations find interest and relevance in my very niche experiences.

When not speaking, I often work as a polar instructor, and throughout 2011 I travelled back and forth to Iceland to conduct training expeditions for clients with increasing regularity. Iceland, being just south of the Arctic Circle, is a popular polar training ground because its glaciers (some of the largest in Europe) remain snow covered well into summer. And yet, late in the season that year it was surprisingly warm as I arrived in Iceland for another training trip, even though it was almost midnight. The sun was still in the sky and everything looked startlingly fresh and green in the lowlands around the airport. My polar equipment needed for the training, packed tightly within two sledges and swaddled in bubble wrap, looked ridiculously out of place in the summery surroundings. As I wheeled the sledges through Reykjavik airport on a baggage trolley they caught the attention of a customs official.

'What is it?' he asked, nodding towards the body-shaped package.

'It's a sledge,' I replied as nonchalantly as possible.

Without a word he waved me on my way, clearly satisfied that I was just a harmless loony rather than a serious threat to national security.

An Icelandic colleague met me at the airport in his outrageously large orange truck with wheels the size of circular hay bales. When my substantial sledges were loaded into the back they looked like nothing more than children's toys.

Driving into Reykjavik we talked about my nascent expedition and that's when I heard about Valdi, a local barber. Not only does he (apparently) give an excellent haircut but he had also been a driver on the Moon Regan Transantarctic Expedition the previous year which had taken modified Ford 6x6 trucks across Antarctica from one coast to the other. The expedition had used a glacier called the Leverett to travel from the central plateau of the continent down onto the Ross Ice Shelf. I tracked the Leverett down on a map, a tiny zigzag of ice tucked into the very top left-hand corner of the Ross Ice Shelf. A bit of research revealed that it was part of the route used by the South Pole Operations Traverse (SPOT), a tractor train that travels from the American base McMurdo on the coast of Antarctica to the South Pole.

This convoy of huge belted vehicles transports 100,000 gallons of fuel and 20,000 lb of cargo on each trip as well as towing large cabins on sledge runners that serve as living accommodation for the staff that drive and maintain the vehicles – a sort of heavy-duty Antarctic caravan. With a top speed of just 10 mph the tractor train is a slow and steady operation taking some thirty days to make the journey one way. The SPOT traverse had become an annual endeavour in recent years and I read stories of four-day blizzards, huge machines completely submerged in snow that set as hard as concrete and winds so strong that it was impossible to leave the safety of the cabin-caravans. Every account of the traverse I could find revealed a tough journey. Ground Penetrating Radar was used to detect crevasses and two tractors were needed to drag each load individually up the steepest parts of the Leverett Glacier. Even so, I was encouraged. If it was possible for these mechanical behemoths to find a route across the Leverett then surely a lone skier would be able to do the same?

The only map of the Leverett I could find showed several crevassed areas, particularly around the head of the glacier where the ice spilled down from the plateau, but very little detail. It was hard to tell exactly what I might expect in terms of snow conditions and gradient. If it was possible for me to ski up the glacier with fully loaded sledges, I would be able to start my traverse from the Ross Ice Shelf side of the continent. Valdi, the Reykjavik barber, was one of only a handful of people on the planet who had travelled on the Leverett, so I was eager to speak to him, hopeful that he might be able to provide some of the answers I needed.

It was already getting dark as my Icelandic friend drove me through a quiet Reykjavik suburb and helped me track down the right address. The houses were warmly inviting, light spilling from their windows or trussed in swarms of fairy-lights around doorways. Leaving the car, we walked a short distance before standing expectantly on a wide porch facing a large front door. I felt oddly nervous as I pressed the doorbell. Valdi answered almost immediately. He was in his late fifties with a softly ageing face, shaven head and glasses. Welcoming us into his spacious open-plan home, it wasn't long before we had spread maps of Antarctica over the dining-room table and were looking at pictures from his expedition over glasses of beer.

'It was very cold at the Pole and we had very bad weather,' he remembered. 'We stopped a few days from the glacier because it was too windy and stayed in that place for quite a while before the weather improved.'

His photographs depicted incredible mountainscapes draped in snow which crumpled like starched linen as it tumbled down the sides of the crags. Of most interest were pictures of the entrance to the Leverett Glacier, an easily missed gap in a seemingly continuous barricade of mountains, but there were limited images of the glacier itself. The few Valdi had taken showed a near-perfect surface of smooth hard snow.

'We didn't see any crevasses on the glacier, not one,' he told me. 'We saw plenty on the valley sides but none at all on the glacier itself.'

This was reassuring news. If a heavy six-wheeled truck had not been bothered by hidden crevasses, it was even less likely that I would have any trouble on skis. Unfortunately, Valdi wasn't able to be so confident when I asked about the gradient of the glacier. The weather had closed in as the team had reached the steepest sections of ice, making it difficult to judge the severity of the slope. He fell silent for a while, thinking over what he could remember. I had only known Valdi for a few hours but there was a quiet surety in his tone that made me trust his judgement. 'I don't think you will have a problem skiing up this glacier,' he said finally.

I nodded my appreciation of his appraisal, fully aware of how difficult it must have been for him to express such a critical opinion when he knew what importance I would attach to it. We fell into a companionable silence, each of us looking at the map on the table, lost in our private thoughts. I stared at the contours of the Leverett and knew: this was my route across Antarctica.

I had just one remaining reservation. The SPOT route on the Leverett was regularly referred to as a 'road' or a 'highway'. Although this was a misleading exaggeration (there was no paving or even piste-ing along the route), if I chose to travel the glacier it was likely I would see some evidence of the convoy and perhaps even some physical markers that had been left behind. This didn't bother me so much from an aesthetic viewpoint but I knew that it would be a reason for my expedition to be belittled by others, particularly within the polar community. Despite this, the plan which had remained a rough idea for years had now, within the space of a few months, transformed into a viable prospect. Returning from Iceland, I realised that it was time to give my proposal the ultimate test – I needed to put it in front of Steve.

Steve works for Antarctic Logistics and Expeditions (ALE), one of only two operators that provide flights into and around Antarctica for expeditions. For the past five years he had been the manager of ALE's Antarctic basecamp. He's seen expeditions come and go, succeed and fail; a level of experience that makes his opinion highly sought after. I knew him as someone who could be relied upon to give a brutally realistic assessment of any expedition plan.

The day I went to see Steve at his home, the forested hills of the Cotswolds were such a vibrant green that they seemed to glow. The sunlight was tinged with lime as it filtered through the new season's leaves that flashed past my open car windows. Summery tunes played on the radio as I swooped along narrow country lanes that plunged and twisted between the hills. Eventually, the curtly polite voice of my satnav told me I had arrived and I pulled up outside a stone building perched on a slope surrounded by beautiful views of the English countryside.

Steve met me at his door, smiling as always. The last time I'd seen him he'd been stood on a wind-scoured runway made of blue ice beneath the Ellsworth Mountains in Antarctica. Today, we made ourselves comfortable with mugs of coffee in his carpeted study which was neatly cluttered with shelves full of polar-themed books and maps of Antarctica. With a large map spread on the floor we were soon squinting at the narrow trickles of white spanning the chain of the Transantarctic Mountains, trying to pinpoint the Leverett. The glacier was so tiny that it was barely visible. I told him the reasons for my choice and my reservations about following the SPOT route.

'Every expedition is following waypoints of one kind or another,' responded Steve, pondering the issue. 'Even Scott was following Shackleton's route. If you took the Axel Heiberg you would still be following waypoints – effectively someone else's route.'

He glanced down at the map, sipping from his mug as he considered my plan.

'I think you're absolutely right, taking on the Axel Heiberg alone is serious stuff. The Leverett is interesting; no one else has skied it before and it looks like a nice route.'

I felt relieved at Steve's tentative approval but at the same time noticed a fizz of trepidation. The plan that had been confined to my imagination was now taking on a reality of its own, as if I had wound a spinning top and was about to let it go.

'I'll try and find out when the SPOT convoy is likely to be on the glacier,' Steve continued. 'In any case, we should probably let them know that you'll be out there. They won't be expecting any skiers.'

He looked at me suddenly and I felt vaguely scrutinised, unable to decipher his expression.

'Not many people have traversed Antarctica by themselves. I'm pretty sure you'll be the first woman at least.'

I nodded in silence, unsure if this was a warning or encouragement. In fact I had already done some careful research and knew full well that only two people had crossed Antarctica alone, both of them men and – significantly – both of them Norwegian. Given the reputation of Norwegians for being excellent skiers, resilient polar experts and legendary explorers, neither fact seemed to bode well for my chances of success. In total, my prospective route would be around 1,700 kilometres and I estimated that it would take me seventy days if I incorporated a bit of time to allow for bad weather or delays. Both of the Norwegians who had crossed Antarctica alone had used kites and parasails but had chosen much longer routes. They'd also made the journeys completely unsupported, towing everything that they needed for their entire expedition in their sledges right from the start. In contrast, I had the opportunity to arrange for at least one resupply along my route, possibly two.

I wasn't sure what worried me more; skiing 1,700 kilometres or spending two months alone. None of the dozen or so expeditions I had completed over the previous ten years equated to what I was about to take on. In terms of distance, the closest I had come was a double crossing of the Greenland ice cap in 2006. My team of four had covered 1,100 kilometres on skis in little over a month. But when it came to surviving as a team of one, I had very little experience. During brief spells working as a guidebook writer I had travelled by myself to some remote corners of the world and back at home I would think nothing of taking myself off on camping trips, walking alone in the hills for days at a time, but these brief periods in my own company were very different from the prospect of my first solitary polar expedition. I would be far more isolated and for a much longer period of time than ever before. I was haunted by a conversation I'd had some months previously with an extremely knowledgeable friend at the Royal Geographical Society who advises almost everyone on every aspect of all types of expeditions. Sitting in the historic brick building of the Society surrounded by wood panelling, shelves of leather-bound books of exploration and the smell of ageing chart paper, I talked about my expedition plans. When I mentioned going alone her reaction was immediate.

'Oh no, Felicity. Don't go alone. I've seen so many wonderful people set off by themselves and they are never quite the same again. It is hard to explain but they always come back different and it is never a change for the better.'

The thought that I might be altered in some way beyond my control was an unnerving one. Every expedition, just like any life experience, influences my character and my future-self but now I considered the possibility of a potentially negative and unwelcome legacy. It made the psychological aspect of the expedition even more daunting.

Past expeditions had taught me so much, first about teamwork and later about leadership, that I was sure this expedition, too, would have its own revelations to impart, particularly regarding the absence of a team. When I thought back on past expedition experiences it was clear to me that I had always drawn much of my motivation and resilience from those around me. It was often the knowledge that I couldn't let my team down that drove me forwards when times were tough. Now that I was to be alone, what would stop me giving up? What would be my incentive to keep going when every muscle and bone wanted to give in? If I sat quietly and closed my eyes I could put myself back in a cold, draughty tent with the noise of the weather outside loud in my ears. I could recall vividly the sense of inertia that comes with mental and physical exhaustion, and remember how easy it is in that moment to convince yourself that it is rational to stay inside a little longer, perhaps sensible to spend an extra hour in your sleeping bag or that an additional rest day is not only deserved but entirely wise. I could see that being alone would make it very easy to allow myself false excuses.

Previously it had always been the presence of a team that had stopped me caving in to these mental vices. A mix of pride and stubbornness would make me determined not to be the weak link in the group. When leading a team I had always been aware of my responsibility to those I was leading to be the best I could be. It was knowing the impact my actions and behaviour would have on others that stopped me falling apart. I wanted to identify what it was that would motivate me to keep going when there was no one to witness my weaknesses.

As I made final preparations for Antarctica, Britain was experiencing an unseasonal heat wave. It was October but the temperatures were soaring as high as 30°C – a return to summer. Wearing a light T-shirt and tracksuit trousers I dragged two heavy car tyres onto the street and attached them to a harness around my waist with a long rope, to mimic pulling a sledge. With an old ski pole clenched in each fist I set off away from my front door towards the sea. I'm fortunate to live close to the coast, and within a few hundred metres I was on a wide concrete path with crumbling chalk cliffs on my left and the brown waves of the English Channel on my right. This was my habitual training route. The path eventually opens out onto the wide sandy arc of Minnis Bay, my favourite stretch. Normally the bay is deserted at this time of year and I would be alone with the dog-walkers and worm-diggers; but today my heart sank. The beach was as crowded as an August weekend with families making the most of the unexpected dose of sunshine. Inwardly bracing myself, I continued along the concrete promenade past the barbeques and sunbathers.

I knew that a woman dragging two car tyres behind her was likely to cause some curiosity but the tyres caught up discarded pebbles which grated loudly against the concrete pathway and dramatically announced my arrival. It was embarrassing to inflict my jarring racket on innocent beach-goers and to be attracting such marked attention to myself. I noticed two elderly ladies walking towards me. One was already open-mouthed in astonishment at the sight approaching her. At first I kept my eyes fixed to the ground but it was impossible to ignore her as I passed. She stared at me, stammering in her inability to formulate a question that encompassed everything she wanted to know all at once. Before she managed to find a place to start, her companion pulled her away.

'I know exactly who you are,' said the companion, with a wink. 'And all about what you are preparing to do. Good luck.'

There had been an article about my preparation in the local paper the previous week and as I moved off I could hear the lady launching into an explanation to her still flabbergasted friend.

It felt strange to have people know about the expedition – as if a big personal secret had been accidentally let out of the bag. It happened again a few days later. I signed for a parcel at the door of my apartment and the postman asked, 'Are you that explorer?'

I looked at him blankly for a second, wondering how he could possibly know. Then I realised that in the entranceway behind me a sledge and a pair of skis were propped against the wall and a large kit bag was spilling an assortment of goggles, jackets and boots over the floor. To get to the doorbell he'd had to step over a large box of fuel bottles and cooking pots.

'Yes, I guess so,' I answered with a smile.

'Ah, thought as much,' he said. 'Well, good luck.'

He handed me my post and was gone.

One of the letters in my hand was marked 'Open on the 31st October'. It was the date I was to leave for Antarctica and I recognised the handwriting; it was from my sister. Overcoming the urge to look inside immediately, I tucked it safely out of sight in my luggage.

When the day of departure arrived I deliberately tried to avoid as many goodbyes as possible. I think I was scared that if I let myself feel nervous or upset I might not be able to regain control. I wanted to fool myself into thinking that I was simply going away on just another trip. The deception seemed to make my nerves easier to handle but by midnight I found myself on the first stop of my journey to Antarctica, sitting alone in the airport terminal at Madrid feeling utterly miserable. Surrounded by strangers, I don't think I had ever felt more isolated. This was only the first stage in a very long journey and yet I already seemed to be an incredibly long way from home. As the countdown to my departure had diminished from weeks to days and finally to hours, I had increasingly felt like a swimmer clinging to the side of a boat over a deep ocean.

I knew that as soon as I launched myself away from safety I would need to be relentlessly focused on simply keeping afloat – never able to stop, never able to relax. It was an intimidating thought but now I found that I'd clamped down so hard on any emotion that I could barely feel anything at all. I could sense myself gradually shutting down, inwardly tensing until I was completely focused on the challenges ahead. It was like a deliberate shedding of everything that was me and replacing it with an altogether more calculated mental state. I was aware of myself being smothered by several layers of self-control and realised glumly that this would be the extent of my inner landscape for the next three months.

Waiting at the boarding gate for my flight I remembered the package from my sister. Inside was a small oval locket made of silver. It opened up to reveal a tiny family photograph opposite a picture of just the two of us laughing at the camera as we share a joke. Sandwiched between the photographs was a thin strip of paper delicately folded to fit the miniscule space.

'Every time you feel alone open this so you know I am with you,' it said. 'All my love from lil' sis.'

I was in tears before I finished reading the note. With blurred vision, I refolded the strip of paper and closed the locket. On the back was engraved:

Every

Step

X

It was beautiful. I ran my fingers over the locket's smooth curves and held it tight in my palm as I boarded the plane.

CHAPTER TWO

PAYING ATTENTION

By late November I should have been well into the first fortnight of my expedition with the Leverett Glacier already behind me but instead I was sitting in ALE's basecamp at Union Glacier looking at the Ellsworth Mountains. It was a clear day and even though the temperature was well below zero it felt warm in the sunshine. I took a mug of coffee from the mess tent and sat on the veranda outside, leaning against the tent wall where it was sheltered from the wind.

Union Glacier is nestled in the heart of the Ellsworths and I let my gaze run over the crowded skyline as I used to do at Rothera. The mountains were different in character to those of my past Antarctic home. Here there was more spike and less curve, and the exposed rock was paler, almost metallic, in the blanching sunlight. I watched the comings and goings in camp, occasionally nodding greetings to passersby heavily wrapped in layers of down. Lifting my face towards the sun I registered once again the irony of the perfect weather above me. For the past ten days I had woken up in a comfortably worn hostel in South America expecting to fly to Antarctica only to be told each morning that a tenacious weather system sat stubbornly over the Ellsworth Mountains preventing all flights. Now that, finally, I had made it to the ice, the bad weather had moved to the Ross Ice Shelf making it impossible to fly to the start point of my expedition.

The delays were more than simply frustrating; they had a serious potential consequence for the success of my expedition. The summer season in Antarctica, the only time of year it is warm and light enough for travel, is extremely short, beginning in November and ending in January. I had a ninety-day window of opportunity in which to complete my seventy-day journey but with each day of delay, that window got a little smaller. Already behind schedule, if I was going to have time to ski all the way across Antarctica I couldn't waste a moment. Perhaps I would have to settle for a lesser goal from the start. As I struggled to remain philosophical about this potential scenario only one thing was clear – for now there was very little I could do except wait.

Despite the delays, I noticed with relief that my desire to disappear over the horizon alone was as strong as ever. Sitting comfortably watching the mountains I was battling with an internal restlessness, a longing to leave everyone and everything behind, to immerse myself completely in the white world beyond the confines of the camp. The craving to sweep across those smooth white surfaces, to skim over the flawless scenery, was as compelling as it had been all those years ago at Rothera.

Not that I wasn't apprehensive. One morning as I sat in the entrance of my tent, lacing up the same ski boots I would be wearing for the journey, I got a flash of that sense of inertia I'd often felt in the past when preparing to begin a day of skiing. I stopped and listened to the wind whining through guy ropes and the snow scratching along the side of the tent as it was blown along the ground in drifts. I closed my eyes and made a mental effort to remember what it is like to ski into that wind all day; to feel numb and exhausted, to feel the pressure of all the miles yet to cover. I hoped this imagined reconstruction would limit the shock when I was finally out there for real.

Others waiting at the basecamp vented their restive nerves by climbing nearby peaks, kite-skiing along the runway or exploring local ranges but I deliberately shied away from doing the same. My reasons were partly practical – I didn't want to risk hurting myself in the days immediately before departure – but there was another less easily explained logic. I felt as if I had focused myself on the journey ahead to the point that it obscured all else; as if I didn't have the mental capacity to think about anything but what lay ahead. Waiting felt like I had freeze-framed myself; a stasis that would only thaw once I was on my way. I had mentally hibernated.

A full fourteen days after I should have started my expedition I heard footsteps approaching my tent. It was Steve. Finally, it was my turn to leave Union Glacier.

I expected the news to fill me with excitement and adrenalin but as I gathered together the last of my belongings and took down my tent I felt the same taut numbness that had gradually enveloped me since leaving the UK. I dragged my sledges, one at a time, over to the small ski plane that was to fly me across Antarctica to my start point.

The narrow but bulky blue sledges that had seemed so large and ungainly next to my tent now appeared pathetically tiny beside the plane. Having chosen to use smaller, plastic sledges I found I couldn't fit the sheer volume of equipment I needed into one alone. Instead I had two identical sledges connected in series with a custom-made pivot. They looked more like a child's toboggan than a serious bit of polar equipment – but looks can be deceptive. I had used similar sledges on nearly all my previous polar expeditions and found that as well as being extremely tough, they had two other advantages over the better looking fibreglass versions: they are lighter and much, much cheaper.

The two pilots loaded the sledges and my skis into the back of the plane. On top I piled the two separate bags I had prepared as resupplies; one I would collect at the South Pole and the second would be left on the ice at a place called Thiels Corner about halfway between the Pole and the end of my journey.

After a few brief goodbyes, I climbed into my seat. It was the only seat on the aircraft and it was right at the back, as far from the pilots as it was possible to get. I felt faintly ridiculous as I strapped myself in, as if I was at the end of a long tunnel, or deliberately quarantined. The pilots twisted round in their seats at the front to give me the thumbs-up before the engines started. I stared out of the window as we jolted down the skiway, watching Union Glacier shrink to become a series of tiny dark blobs on the snow, before being engulfed completely by the panorama that expanded as we gained height. From above, the mountains looked like misshapen starfish partly covered with fine white sand, ridges and arêtes splayed out like short stubby tentacles.

The plane banked sharply and we headed south, flying between the larger peaks. I struggled to pick out features of the landscape that had been particularly striking from the ground but which were now almost lost in the flattened view from the air. Eventually, I recognised the broad, rounded hump of Patriot Hills sitting slightly apart from the rest of the mountain range and used it as a reference to guide my gaze and pick out Three Sails, a row of snow-smothered nunataks (the tips of mountains that have been otherwise submerged by ice) which resembled evenly spaced pimples. As I looked down at the lumpy shadows they cast I reflected that if all went well I would be skiing past those same outcrops in some two months' time. By that stage I would be covering the very last miles of my journey, the trio of distinctive peaklets acting as a signpost to direct me to the nearby coast. I tried to imagine what it would feel like to be that future version of myself and what would be going through my mind after weeks alone, knowing that a thousand miles lay behind me.

Three Sails gradually glided out of view beyond the scope of my scratched and distorted porthole in the side of the plane and I was left with a blinding glare of white. Pulling my sunglasses down over my eyes I still had to squint to pick out surface texture on the endless plain below. It wasn't smooth but covered in a web of corrugations, reminding me of the intricate formations of an organism magnified under a microscope. At first the grain of the ground looked to be totally random but then I began to detect a regularity in its pattern, as if a single motif was being repeated over and over. Lines and scores, smooth patches and regular parallels. From the air it looked as harmless as the crinkles on a ruffled shirt but I wondered how different the perspective from the ground would be.

The plane flew on and on over mile after mile of the same pleated expanse. There was no end to its span and no variation in its character. It seemed impossible that I could expect to ski across such vastness. I couldn't help laughing at my own naivety but I was struck by the sheer enormity of the distance I was taking on. One thousand seven hundred kilometres sounded like a lot on paper but now that I was seeing it for real, every inch, I was left in no doubt. It was a very long way by plane; it was an inconceivable distance by foot. I became aware of a growing reverberation deep in my belly but I couldn't tell if it was simply the tremor of the plane's engines. There were nerves but there was also – at last – a welling excitement. I could feel the freedom of striking out across those drifts, imagine the searing cold that would make me feel ecstatically alive and sense the satisfaction of marching towards an empty horizon.

The small plane had set off with full tanks, but still had to stop not once but twice to refuel in order to reach the far side of the continent. The second stop was high on the Antarctic plateau quite a way to the west of the route I would be taking. I climbed out of the back of the plane to stretch my legs while the pilots pumped sharp-smelling aviation fuel direct from squat black oil drums propped upright in the snow. The wind sent long streams of drift skidding along the ground toward the horizon as if all the loose material in Antarctica was being sucked northwards. It was far colder than it had been at Union Glacier because we were much higher. I squinted into the wind until my cheeks went numb, then turned and scanned the view in the opposite direction. The sky was choked with broad brushstrokes of cloud that flattened the light. Each layer had its own subtly different shade, giving the overall effect of gleaming like mother-of-pearl. Distracted by the sky, I almost missed a dark shadow resting on the horizon, an irregular pyramid of hazy grey, and then a whole chain of them stretching right the way across the distant view. It was my first sight of the Transantarctic Mountains.

The pilots finished refuelling and climbed into the plane. One of them shouted back to me,

'You explorers are true rock stars to voluntarily spend time out here. I can't imagine being out in conditions like this.'

I laughed with him but the truth was I could barely imagine it either and had been as grateful as anyone else to scuttle back into the relative warmth and shelter of the aircraft. Standing out in the wind, my body had recoiled in shock from the cold and yet in just a few weeks I would be back on the plateau and these conditions would be the reality of my daily existence.

It wasn't long before we were suspended high above the mountains I had seen from the ground. The tops of the ridges on the lower hills were almost bare of snow, the rock showing through like wrack lines of tide-washed debris on a white sand beach. Between them were wide channels of ice, the moraine and rock debris trapped within each glacier visible as fine dark trails along their length. Carried steadily but imperceptibly slowly downwards through the mountains, these moraine trails mark out the movement of the glaciers in long, delicate stripes as orderly and sinuous as hand-carved arabesques. This graceful dance of ice and rock stretched on in all directions so that my eyes darted around the landscape struggling to take it in. I pressed my forehead against the plastic glass of the aircraft window, straining to get the widest possible field of view. Then I noticed soft scars radiating outwards from the top of the nearest glaciers; perfectly concentric impressions of hundreds of snow-covered crevasses in an otherwise creamy surface. They looked like the ripples on the surface of a pool, only inverted, the snow sagging slightly into the fissures it covered like a sheet of silk.

It was beautiful but terrifying; the very essence of sublime. I couldn't help but imagine the horror of trying to pick a route through such a minefield. It was impossible to tell from the air how big the fissures were but as the shadow of the plane flittered across their contours it regularly disappeared completely into the blackness of gaping holes where the snow had fallen through to leave yawing voids. In a second, the reverberations in the pit of my stomach had solidified into a leaden mass. I felt like I'd been winded and the sensation made me cough. I tore my eyes from the window and stared hard at my feet as I fought the rising panic. Was this the top of the Leverett Glacier? Would I have to ski across this confusion of crevasses? Was this what I had condemned myself to? The mass in my stomach became so heavy that its gravity seemed to pin me to the spot, like the nauseating sensation of looping the loop on a roller coaster.

My brain's first instinct was to search for an escape. It would be perfectly justifiable, I reasoned with myself, to return to Union Glacier and explain that after seeing what I would be facing I'd realised I wasn't up to it. I'd rather accept what others might see as the humiliation of bailing out than end up dead. I recalled stories I'd been told of people who had prematurely ended expeditions by citing dubious injury or tenuous logistical complications as an excuse to go home and I felt a sudden flood of sympathy. In that Damascene moment any sense of derision was replaced with total understanding.

As the flood of panic subsided, I remembered the thrill of freedom I had anticipated not a few hours before as the plane had flown over the endless patterns of the plateau, and my tremors were replaced with defiance. I wanted to stay, I wanted to camp, I wanted to be out there. Cautiously I got out of my seat and moved around the unsteady aircraft, peering through different windows in an attempt to get my bearings. I tried to match the flattened view of the mountains to what I could remember of my map. Away to the right was a vast corridor of ice that I reasoned must be the Reedy Glacier. I knew the Reedy was the last in the series of ice-routes across the Transantarctic Mountains and as I could see no other glaciers beyond the snaking ice-river below, I took it as my best guess. Working my way to the left I figured that on the other side of the rock barrier almost beneath the plane's wing must be the Leverett. Anxiety bubbled in my veins like soda as I willed the plane onwards to a better vantage point and my first glimpse of the Leverett Glacier, but as soon as we moved high enough over the intervening peaks to see beyond, the tiny aircraft was enveloped in cloud. I strained at the range of my restricted view through the windows to spot any gap in the cloud – then suddenly it was there.

Beneath me, unmistakably, was the Leverett Glacier.

It looked even smaller in actuality than it had on the maps. A tiny channel of white, sandwiched between tall barriers of rock. I stared fixated, burning the image into my memory. Ice clung to the sides of the peaks channelling the glacier in cataracts of irregular blocks, but there were no frightening rib cages of crevasses to be seen. It looked far more manageable than any of the other sweeping glaciers we had flown over and distinctly less terrifying. As I looked, I noticed a tiny dark thread running along the centre of the glacier, ending in a series of dark specks. At first I was confused, then I realised what I was looking at; it was the SPOT traverse. The specks were the vehicles and the dark thread was their track. I only saw it for an instant before the cloud once again isolated the plane from the view below but I sank back in my seat grappling with the consequences of what I had just seen.

I had hoped to start my expedition significantly before the SPOT traverse was due so that I would be making a fresh trail. Due to the weather delays, it appeared I would be following the traverse instead. If the vehicles were already on the glacier, the convoy would be far enough ahead of me that I wouldn't see them at any point but would I see evidence that they had passed through? I realised with resignation that whatever the outcome, it was out of my hands and I would have to adjust my expectations to fit whatever I found.

The next time the cloud cleared we had flown on past the narrow strait of the Leverett and were heading towards the coast.

Antarctic coastlines are notoriously elusive and controversial. The main problem is that the thick layer of ice that covers the continent flows from land onto the sea and forms huge floating platforms called Ice Shelves. The coast is the point at which grounded ice over land becomes floating ice over water but from the surface it is impossible to tell the difference as both look and feel the same. Only by referring to maps can the coastline be identified and, lacking detailed data, the maps represent a kind of geologic best guess rather than a scientific certainty.

Far beneath the wings of the plane, ice that had crept at minute speeds from the plateau at the heart of the continent trickled through gaps in the Transantarctic Mountains as winding glaciers. Like rivers emptying into a delta, they drained out onto the wide expanse of the Ross Ice Shelf to form an immense platform of floating ice that stretched northward from the feet of the Transantarctic Mountains to open water somewhere way beyond the horizon.

Below, I could still see the dark thread of the traverse route forging across the snow as level as a ruled line and knew that it continued all the way to McMurdo, the American base some 1,000 kilometres away on the other side of the Ross Ice Shelf. Either side of the tracks I could see the tell-tale dark spokes of crevassing, visible beneath the snow like blue veins under a cadaverous skin. In places the crevasses clustered together in a dense plexus and at times the tracks appeared to be so close as to kiss the outlying fissures as it skimmed by.

We descended over the Ross Ice Shelf, circling the tracks to take a closer look. The convoy had left a series of deep parallel impressions in the snow perhaps as much as ten metres wide in places and it presented the safest option for a crevasse-free landing. The plane, fitted with skis under its wheels, used the imprints as a rough runway and rumbled to an abrupt halt on the ice.

I had already been warned that the pilots would only be shutting down one engine and that they would be leaving as soon as possible. They didn't want to risk getting stuck on the ground so far from home. The door next to my seat opened and the head of one pilot appeared.

'Did you see the crevasses?' he shouted over the noise of the remaining engine.

I nodded emphatically, my eyes wide in a caricature of the alarm I had felt as we had flown over them. The pilot disappeared and the co-pilot replaced him in the doorway, crawling into the back to help me with my sledges.

'Did you see those crevasses?' he asked as we passed each other.

I nodded again and noticed that his face was full of concern. 'Good,' he said solemnly. 'I'm glad you were paying attention.'

With both of my sledges on the snow a few feet from the plane I triple-checked I had everything. The pilots hovered nearby as if reluctant to leave. One took a photo and the other shook my hand, wishing me luck. I tried to hide it but I could already feel the tremble of panic gathering strength inside me. The co-pilot pointed to the snow at my feet.

'You've dropped your glove,' he said.

I snatched it up, embarrassed to have been caught making such an amateur mistake. I was lucky that it hadn't blown away. Stepping back from the plane I stood watching as the idle engine kicked into life. I readied my camera to film the plane leaving but as it lifted into the air and banked back towards me to fly past, I forgot about taking pictures and bounced up and down on the spot waving my arms in great arcs above my head as if the exertion of energy could exorcise the growing feeling of terror in my chest.

Then I stood, motionless, fixing my gaze on the vanishing black smudge in the sky. I could sense the mountains to my left but I barely dared to look at them, as if glancing at my surroundings would make it real and I wasn't ready to face the reality of the moment – not yet. Instead, I stood staring at the sky with a sense of dread as the silence rushed in. It was a tangible, roaring silence that seemed to thicken the air around my head, exerting a pressure on my temples and filling my ears, rushing into my mouth as I tried to breathe. As I moved around my sledges attempting to shepherd my brain into focusing on pitching my tent and organising my equipment, I didn't seem able to shake off the quiet. I felt like a large, noisy, cumbersome interloper on an otherwise perfectly blended landscape. I found myself moving unnecessarily softly as if frightened of disturbing the calm around me. Every instinct tightened to the point that I felt brittle, as if a sudden movement would crack my bones.

Pitching my tent took twice as long as it should have done. In an effort to distract myself from the emotional turmoil in my chest I went through my routine with unusual attention to detail, making sure every anchor was perfectly secure, every guy rope symmetrically placed and as taut as a tightrope. The tent was a dark green Hilleberg, specifically designed for extreme expeditions. Inside, it had two areas; a deep vestibule at one end by the entrance that I used for cooking, and a zipped canary-yellow sleeping compartment at the other end that was just long enough for me to lie down stretched out without pressing my toes against the back of the tent. It was tall enough that I could sit cross-legged in the very centre without touching the inner lining but sufficiently narrow to be able to stretch out my arms and place my palms flat to each of the sides.

Eventually I crawled into the yellow and green shade of my little shelter but spent longer than necessary carefully placing all my belongings where they were designed to be in the two compartments. When I was done the tent was snug but somehow I couldn't see it as cosy. I was too aware of what was missing, too sensitive to the emptiness and the quiet. I had a meal to cook but the very thought of food made me feel sick – my nerves were still quivering in my stomach and the tension made it feel bloated and full. I glanced at my watch and realised that it was almost midnight even though the sun was still radiating brightly through the side of the tent. Grabbing one of my colour-coded bags I took out my satellite phone and switched it on. It was no bigger than my hand but was now my only contact with the world.

There were two calls I would make every day: one to Union Glacier to report my position, and the other to an automated 'phonecast' service. A phonecast is exactly like a podcast except it is made by calling a number from a phone and recording a message – like leaving a voicemail. The message is then automatically uploaded onto the expedition website so that anyone can instantaneously listen to me describing my progress. I planned to record a message every day so that those who wanted to follow my expedition could hear directly from me about how things were going, but it was an entirely one-way form of communication.

I dialled the number as I thought about what I wanted to say. I wasn't sure that I was capable in that moment of being very eloquent. I was barely able to digest and understand the thoughts running through my brain, never mind translate them into words and package them into sentences. Regardless, I was aware that a lot of people would be eagerly awaiting my news and so I had to record something, even if it was just the bare facts of my arrival. Those who were most likely to listen to the message were friends, family and my parents as well as sponsors and the media, so I tried to sound as positive as possible, describing the scene around me and my excitement to be there. I didn't mention the dreadful sense of alone-ness or the instinctive terror that made me feel nauseous. It was easy to sound deliberately upbeat for the few minutes of the recording but the cheer I could hear in my voice didn't reflect what I was feeling. After hanging up, the silence crept back in, like water collecting in rock pools as the tide returns.

I stared in silence at the satellite phone in my lap for a long time. Theoretically I could have called anybody in the world from my tent but I realised sadly that no one could help me with the mental shock of being alone. I was on my own in more than just the physical sense and somehow I had to process that fact. I had to get past the reflex of fear. Until I had my emotions under control I didn't feel I had the capacity to share what I was going through with anyone. Instead I texted a single word in an SMS message to the expedition Twitter account. It read simply, 'Alone.'

I switched off the satphone and put it away. Wriggling into my sleeping bag, squirming until I was comfortable, I lay unmoving, listening to the quiet. I tried not to think of the challenge to come, of the weight of the miles and days ahead.

Before leaving the UK I'd tried to prepare for this moment by seeking the help of a sports psychologist. Dr Pack is a research scientist with an interest in solitude and psychological resilience as well as how this might be linked to particular thought or mood patterns and processes. The first time we spoke was over the phone. He talked in rapid bursts followed by long silences but the conversation was encouraging. Despite the fact that most of his work had focused on high-performing athletes dealing with the mental stress of competition and training, many of the issues I raised seemed to be familiar to him. He told me that the next stage would be something he called 'mental deconstruction'. I wasn't sure that I wanted to be 'deconstructed' but he assured me that it was just a matter of understanding my thought processes better. We met a few weeks later at the University. He was a small, slight man who listened intently as I explained my worries about the expedition to come. As I spoke I tried to organise my thoughts into some kind of order but ended up rambling about everything from homesickness to hallucinations. Given the randomness of my monologue I was a little surprised when he was able to put scientific labels on most of my anxieties. I found it fascinating that what I considered to be my own personal foibles were actually recognisable consequences of the way our brains work.

One of my biggest worries was if, through isolation, exhaustion or general mental disorientation, I would no longer be able to rely on my own brain to make reasonable, considered choices. For example, I'd learnt through experience that one of the first signs that someone may be getting too cold and slipping into hypothermia is that they start behaving strangely. They might become uncharacteristically quiet, wear a jacket they don't normally need, be incoherent, or be clumsy in their movements. It's not uncommon for people with severe hypothermia to be convinced that they are too hot and start removing clothing even though their life may depend on them doing the exact opposite. What scared me is that it is never the person affected who notices the changes in their behaviour. It is those travelling with them that detect the signs. In my case, there was no one with me to pick up on the fact that I was making inappropriate decisions. How would I know if I was making a decision for the right reasons?

In answer, Dr Pack had introduced me to 'Resilient Thinking'; the process of analysing thoughts and decisions in order to understand the driving emotions behind them. It was a way of checking up on myself, of making a conscious effort to examine every decision to ensure that I was being objective. I could see the value of the process but it sounded exhausting. Lying in my tent on that first day alone in Antarctica I tried analysing the fear that still lurked behind every thought, but found myself being distracted by the slightest of sounds around me. There was the soft hiss of snow being blown along the ground and against the side of the tent, the tap of a loose thread brushing against taut tent fabric, the crackle of my sleeping bag around my ears. Drowning out all else was the roar of the stillness. The longer I lay listening, the greater the pitch of the silence. It built steadily, filling my ears, vibrating in my head until it reached a crescendo and I could bear it no more.

'Go Away!' I bellowed from my sleeping bag.

My irrational outburst seemed to help, as if the sound of my own voice had broken a spell. I got comfortable again and concentrated on remembering the sounds that had surrounded me at Union Glacier, attempting to fool myself into thinking I was still in the middle of a basecamp. In my mind I transformed the noises of the wind into the faint snores of sleeping teams in tents nearby and mutated the regular beat of my blood pumping through my ears into the mechanical clamour of a bulldozer. It seemed to work; at least, I woke to find the sun on the opposite side of the tent and realised that I had slept.

CHAPTER THREE

LOO-JW

@felicity_aston With the first step of my journey I start the long road home...

@felicity_aston Got woken several times by low flying jet planes last night. Then remembered no planes in Antarctica. It was the wind.

@felicity_aston Struggling this morning.

As I opened my eyes on that first morning alone in Antarctica, I could feel my mind swinging rapidly between sentimental despair and numb practicality. I attempted to implement some resilient thinking but marshalling my rampaging emotions seemed to require too much energy and I quickly gave up. I moved around the small shelter, zipping up bags, packing away items I wouldn't need again that morning as I went and putting on extra layers. I couldn't help but think how different it was to sharing a tent with three other women as I had the last time I skied to the Pole. With everyone playing their part, it had taken little more than an hour from the moment we woke to our departure on skis. Everything took significantly longer now that I was taking care of all the jobs myself. I pulled out my daily food ration and separated the bag of breakfast. Compressed into the bottom corner of the bag was a large handful of oats mixed with generous quantities of sugar and powdered milk, and which was already congealing into a tight ball around the thick knob of butter I'd sliced into each portion. I boiled the water ready to make the oats into porridge but changed my mind at the last minute. My stomach felt bloated with nerves and the thought of food made me want to retch. I forced down some chocolate and stashed the rest of breakfast with my cooking equipment.

Fastening my light windproof jacket and pulling down my goggles I opened the tent door and stepped outside. The glare of the snow made me squint. It was a beautiful day with a solid blue sky and a slight, steady wind. I straightened up and breathed in deeply. The cold air felt fresh and sharp, waking me up as I stood and surveyed the mountains. It was the first time I'd felt brave enough to look at them in detail. They were arranged in front of me like a closely packed battalion. Those at the back were chiselled into spires that stretched for the sky while at their feet smaller hills and nunataks crowded together creating an overlapping pastiche of rock and ice. The rise and fall of the saddled ridges and lower summits resembled the regular ridge and scoop of a scalloped shell.

I was amazed at the bright tones of the rock; while the peaks in the distance were a dusky lilac, those closer by were vibrant ochre. It was more orange than anything I had seen at either Rothera or in the Ellsworths and the colour seemed to leach outward so that the snow beneath them reflected a soft pink. Most impressive of all was the sheer extent of the range. It stretched from horizon to horizon connecting east to west and appeared to be an impenetrable blockade. Any gaps between the summits were filled with immense jumbles of ice that were breathtakingly beautiful and yet radiated a ferocious, hostile menace. I turned slowly trying to take it all in, my breath forming vapour trails in the air. Not many people have the fortune to see these mountains. Gazing on wonder after wonder I could feel a swelling exhilaration that tightened my throat and filled my eyes with tears. Soon I was sobbing in joyous disbelief that I was actually standing on the Ross Ice Shelf looking at the Transantarctic Mountains. It was as if I had been allowed a glimpse of something sacred.

'I'm here!' I shouted to the mountains, laughing.

'I'm here!' I shouted louder, aware that my voice was instantly diluted into nothingness by the space around me.

I shivered in the silence that echoed back.

It was time to move on.

I struck camp and took a picture of my two sledges, now connected one behind the other. The backdrop of mountains seemed to shimmer like a mirage in the harsh blue light. I strapped on my harness for the first time and took a deep breath before pushing forward on my skis. Despite a combined weight of some 85 kg, the sledges glided obediently at my heels with very little resistance.

With the Transantarctic Mountains on my right I took my first steps away from the coast. My route was obvious, I simply had to follow the line of peaks until I found the narrow gap that I had seen from the air with the Leverett Glacier running through it. This would be my gateway up to the higher ground of the Antarctic Plateau. Having flown over the glacier, I knew it was concealed somewhere in the chain of ridges, buttresses and mountainsides that stretched away from me to the east but even if I had been in any doubt of which direction to take, the tracks of the SPOT traverse were unmistakable as they darted ahead of me toward the horizon. I skied clear of them but they were always there, as unshakable as a shadow, dominating the landscape. I tried not to be disappointed by this intrusion of a manmade scar into a place I had expected to be unblemished.

Despite the fact that the ground around me looked as solid as carved granite, the memory of the view I had seen from the air, specifically the dark spectres of crevasses lurking under the snow surface on either side of the tracks, was still vivid in my mind. My heart beat faster when I dwelled on it and instinctively I placed my gloved hand on the cold bulk of the satellite phone in my jacket pocket. Usually I kept the handset safely stowed in my sledge but now that I was travelling alone I wanted it close at hand. If the worst happened and I fell into a crevasse I couldn't be sure that I would be able to reach my sledge. I tried not to think about the fact that the chances of getting a signal on a satellite phone from the bottom of a narrow crack in the ice were pretty remote regardless.

It felt good to be on my way and to feel the familiar rhythm of ski, pole and sledge; breath and heartbeat. The steady wind kept me cool but I could feel the heat of the sun through my thin windproof jacket. The snow surface was softly scored by the wind into low, snaking ridges but it was flat enough that I could look around me as I skied without needing to concentrate on the ground. I couldn't keep my eyes off the mountain scenery to my right. Each sweep of my gaze across the buckled skyline picked out delicate details that by themselves were exquisite and together as a whole were almost overwhelming. Occasionally I would look in the opposite direction towards the empty vastness of the Ross Ice Shelf on my left, a clean, featureless horizon precisely dividing dense blue sky from harshly white snow. The contrast with the mountainscape was so absolute that I could have been flitting between two entirely different planets with a simple turn of my head. The Ross Ice Shelf looked desolate and lonely in its flat emptiness, especially in comparison to the chain of peaks which, although silent and devoid of life, did at least fill my world with colour and texture. It was an ominous thought that within a matter of weeks the mountains would be nothing but a memory and I would be surrounded by empty landscape identical to the featureless world of the Ross Ice Shelf.

After skiing several kilometres, I caught sight of a dark scratch in the pale shades up ahead. As I drew closer, glide by glide, the scratch deepened, its edges too straight to be made by nature. Eventually it revealed itself as a tall wooden post hammered into the ground and surrounded by tattered green pennants writhing in the wind on bamboo poles. At the top of the post were engraved the letters, 'LOO-JW'. I took off my skis and walked around the post until I found several signatures in black marker pen, slightly faded on the surface of the heavily grained wood but still clearly visible. Among them I spotted the name Valdi and remembered the man I'd met in Reykjavik who had signed this post almost exactly a year previously.

Placed originally by the SPOT traverse as a navigational marker, LOO-JW had gained significance in recent years as a visible indicator of the Antarctic coast. Located just north of the eighty-fifth line of latitude, the post stood almost exactly over the coastline marked on the few available maps of the region – a coastline that was otherwise completely undetectable from the surface. Nobody seemed to know what the initials 'LOO-JW' carved into the top of the post stood for but Valdi and the Moon Regan Transantarctic Expedition he had been a part of had used it as the endpoint of their transcontinental journey, and so it became the official start of mine. Just to make sure there could be no doubt that I had started my crossing on ice floating on the ocean and not on the Antarctic landmass, the plane had flown me a little further north to be well beyond this unassuming coastal marker.

I balanced my small pocket camera on the top of one of the sledges and posed for a photograph leaning against the LOO-JW post. Looking again at the weathered signatures I fished a black map-marker out of my bags and added my name. I dated it then, after a pause, wrote underneath, 'Alone – On Skis.' I stood back and looked at my signature. It looked brazen in fresh black ink on the muted wood and I felt a flicker of remorse. Scrawling my name had irreversibly announced my presence. I had declared my intentions in brutal black and now there would be no slinking away.

Over the following hours I established the routine that I would follow for the next two months: skiing for ninety minutes before stopping for a short break to eat from a bag of snacks I kept in my pocket and to drink from an insulated water bottle that I kept nested within my down jacket at the front of the leading sledge. The familiarity of the routine – which was very similar to that of past expeditions – soothed some of the unease of the morning and allowed me to be less sensitive to the isolation. Being on the move I felt as comfortable as I ever had on a polar journey.

I kept a close eye on the watch that I wore on the outside of my jacket sleeve. In the austral summer when the sun is in the sky twenty-four hours a day, the passage of time is difficult to judge because the quality of the light never changes. The sun never dips towards the horizon to create the golden light of late afternoon or rises to give the blue light of morning, it simply circles endlessly overhead. The time of day becomes arbitrary because mid-afternoon looks and feels exactly like mid-morning and there is no darkness whatsoever. Some find it disorientating but I found that I preferred permanent daylight to the normal division of day and night. When it was time to sleep I simply pulled the hat I wore to bed over my eyes to simulate darkness but if ever I woke up, it was always bright enough to see.

I could choose any global timezone I wished and could ski as long as I wanted but I had learnt that it was important to be consistent; skipping back and forth between timezones quickly confuses the body and is never a good idea. I needed a regular rhythm and gave myself a specific time to get up each morning and a regular time to stop skiing each day, allowing myself enough sleep to let my body recover. If I was going to keep going right the way across the continent, recuperation was going to be as vital as mileage.

I was in a euphoric mood at the end of that first day but as soon as I crawled into the glaucous world of my small tent the nauseating sense of fear and trembling dread of the silence came flooding back. In my tent there was no hiding from the reality that I was alone. I boiled melted snow to make my dinner, a freeze-dried meal in a foil bag, but I couldn't manage more than a few mouthfuls even though I'd eaten very little during the day. My stomach felt too tense to force in food, as if I was on the brink of being sick. I made myself a hot milky coffee and mixed in some protein powder so it was thick and gloopy. With the mug steaming I spread out my map and marked the position of my camp. It was pleasing to see that the neat black cross was a respectable distance from where I had started. Using my Global Positioning System (GPS) unit I worked out that I had skied nearly fourteen nautical miles (26 kilometres) on my first day – four more than my target. A nautical mile is just a little longer than a more commonly used statute mile and is a more convenient measure of distance when working in latitude and longitude as I was. I made careful notes in my tiny pad, detailing my location and progress as well as the date and the day of the week. I knew from experience that it wouldn't be long before I would lose track of how many days I had been skiing, never mind the date, month or day, unless I kept a reliable record.

I woke on my second morning to turbulent weather, the snow being blown along the ground towards me so that it looked like a layer of smoke. Setting off, the sledge felt heavy and my body seemed wearily reluctant. While skiing I kept my head down, using the hood of my jacket to protect my fleece-covered face from the oncoming wind but when I stopped every couple of hours for a break I'd use the time to study the now familiar array of mountains that hovered at a constant distance to my right. Although I was looking at the same peaks that I had seen on arrival, their appearance gradually altered as I skied. The summit with the multi-spiked crown that had been so distinct on my first morning was now a single hump, its formerly prominent profile lost amongst the serac-scarred shoulders of other mountains. Kelly Nunatak, which had been a dirty smudge at the foot of the peaks ahead, revealed itself, mile by mile, as a heap of dark stone with streaks of rock dust spreading like a stain of black ink in the snow beneath it. Similarly, a feature that had been visible at the start as a small blemish on the horizon gradually grew into Marsh Ridge, a prominent protrusion of vivid auburn rock stretching out from the line of mountains. Its transformation provided a pleasing measure of my progress towards it. Most of my ski journeys in the past had been across featureless plateaus of white so it was a novelty to have such a constant measure of scale and movement.

Each mile brought something new, allowing me to peer between buttresses to see short valleys blocked by cataracts of ice, or glimpse sheer rock faces draped with hanging gardens of snow blocks. It was an endless conveyor belt of natural spectacle. I could feel myself rushing, pushing forward, eager for the next display. I couldn't help my gaze flicking forward, searching the crags for any sign of the narrow corridor that would allow me through the mountains to the plateau beyond. Several times I was sure I could detect a gap, a slight cleft that looked as if it could lead to a route southward, but each time I came upon the head of the suspected corridor it would turn out to be something else. I was taut with impatience even though I knew from my maps that the gap in the mountains used by the Leverett was some twenty kilometres further along and would be beyond my view for at least another day. It was futile to try and predict its place in the pleats of rock. It would appear in its own time.

I diverted my mind to other matters, carefully avoiding all thoughts of home, the journey ahead or anything else that might damage my fragile sense of well-being. Focusing on my surroundings, I noticed how the snow drifting past my feet, propelled by the wind, looked like running water. I was struck by the fancy that I was swimming rather than skiing and amused myself by making breaststroke motions with my arms as I glided forward on my skis, occasionally switching to front crawl or even butterfly. My surreal mime made me smile at my own silliness and I continued to swim into wind past my aquarium of mountains. I found myself humming a tune, then realised that, being alone, I was free to vent my joy in any way I pleased. I bellowed out the tune in my head but as my voice cracked and reverberated off key I decided that even an audience of one was perhaps one too many.

'Thank goodness for that,' I said aloud to the air when I stopped singing.

They were the first words I had spoken all day.

Talking to myself, I noticed, was a completely instinctive response to being alone. When it was time to pitch the tent I found myself giving a running commentary to the space around me,

'Front pegs first,' I instructed as I pinned out the tent in the snow.

'Make them nice and sturdy. There we go.'

'Keep everything tidy. You don't want to lose anything,' I cautioned.

Then when I stood back to survey my work I congratulated myself in satisfaction, 'Tent looks good. Nice job.'

As it had the previous day, my good mood disappeared as soon as I crawled into the tent and I was revisited by the now recognisable pall of loneliness. The nausea returned too, as if it was the physical manifestation of the unease that shivered through every nerve. I forced down my evening meal because I knew how much my body needed the energy, but every mouthful was a struggle. Once again I had eaten hardly anything during the day and as I looked at the bags of food left over from my first forty-eight hours I was conscious of all the missing nutrients it represented and the impact it would have. In the past I had relentlessly nagged my teams to eat every single scrap of each day's allocated food, so it was with a degree of guilt that I hid the excess food from my sight. I knew I had to start eating but I reasoned that perhaps it was ambitious to expect my body to adjust overnight to digesting the 4,500 calories in my daily rations.

At the end of my third day I camped in front of a tall orange mountain with a thick cap of snow on its summit. Its exposed faces were heavily crenulated like the wrinkled skin of an ancient and the rich colour of the rock seemed to glow in the sunlight. Although not the tallest peak, it stood out from the rest of the range, sitting on a corner like a newel post. It made an immediate impression on me and once I had pitched the tent I stood for a while letting my gaze rise upwards over its rutted surface. Pulling the map from my sledge I marked the position of my camp and tried to match the topography on paper to the view in front of me. The magnificent craggy mountain had to be the knot of concentric contours named on the map as Mount Beazley. If so, I realised with mounting excitement, the slope to its left was the narrow stretch of the Leverett Glacier that I had seen from the air, the corridor to the plateau. It was hard to glean much from where I was camped about the route through the gap. The ground looked smooth except for a large area of obvious crevasses near the top showing up against the white like a patch of cracked and peeling paint. It was impossible to deduce anything at all about the gradient. I had skied up several hills in the last few days, the weight of my sledges making each slope a hard, sweat-inducing slog of patience and tiny increments. Yet none of the hills I had encountered so far had been acknowledged on the map with so much as a single contour. In contrast, the rise ahead of me was ominously represented by a cluster of tightly spaced lines.

That evening as I went about my regular routine of chores in the tent, trying to ignore the heavy weight of silence, I became aware of a regular tap of an unseen corner of tent material vibrating in an otherwise quiet wind. The noise became a constant distraction, like the repeated hammering of a drill. Unable to ignore the irritation any longer I threw down the bag in my hands in anger and turned to the source of the noise.

'Shut up!' I yelled.

No sooner had the words escaped me than I was laughing at my own absurdity. First I couldn't stand the stillness and now I was in a fury at the slightest of sounds. In any case the tent continued to flap remorselessly for the rest of the night. I might have enjoyed the relative silence more if I had known that it was to be my last evening of calm for more than a fortnight but as I set off the next morning the weather didn't betray any hint of what was to come. The sun was so hot that I wore nothing but thermals under my padded salopettes and I stopped several times to plaster more suncream onto the tip of my nose which protruded slightly from under my face mask. For the first couple of hours I skied in a gentle arc around the towering flanks of Mount Beazley and then quite suddenly, within the space of no more than a hundred metres, I moved out from behind the shelter of the mountain into a cold and determined wind flowing down the slope of the narrowing glacier ahead.

The change was as abrupt and dramatic as stepping out from the shadows into the full glare of a tropical sun. I knew instantly that this wasn't just a local breeze. This supercooled air belonged to the very centre of Antarctica where temperatures are at their most extreme. Driven by gravity, these southern winds roll downwards from the top of the continent's domed interior towards the coast, tearing over mile after mile of scored and scarred polar wasteland, gathering momentum. Before they can reach the flat expanse of the ice shelf, the winds hit the Transantarctic Mountains which form an almighty barricade between the plateau and the lower altitudes of the coast. The winds hurl themselves at the rock, sweeping along the corrugated escarpments searching for any route through. The invisible surges, frustrated in their quest for the sea, build up behind the blockade of mountains forming tumultuous weather systems (one of which had delayed my start) but eventually they find the chinks between the peaks, like the restricted corridor of the Leverett I now skied towards.

The great volume of air that has travelled so far squeezes itself through these tiny channels with fearsome force. These fulminating winds, governed by gravity rather than by weather systems, are called katabatic. Some of the strongest winds ever recorded on the planet have been katabatic winds in Antarctica. They can persist with immense force for days at a time but are usually very localised, which means that if you don't want to wait out a katabatic storm you should, in theory, be able to travel right through it.

Ahead of me I could see snow rising like clouds of steam from outcrops of rock on either side of the narrow channel I was to pass through, whipped into puffs by unseen winds strong enough to create mini-tornadoes. I stopped to readjust my clothing and prepare for the worsening weather. Closing any tiny gaps in the layers that covered my face and putting on my windproof jacket, I made sure to fasten any pockets or vents that had been left open. It was like getting ready for battle and the enemy was the wind. As I skied onward into worsening gusts I considered my forward strategy.

In principle, katabatic winds would be strongest over the steepest ground but I could expect them to diminish as I reached flatter ground beyond the top of the glacier. Therefore, if I skied far enough, I should have been able to ski right through the bad weather. The problem was I had no idea how far I would have to ski until I reached flatter ground or just how sheer the glacier was going to get. I wasn't even completely sure that these were katabatic winds at all. If it was simply a weather system, the high winds could extend for dozens of kilometres. I had such little information that I gradually accepted there was no strategy to be had except to plunge forward. I felt my face fixing into a grimace of grim determination beneath my face mask as I moved ever closer to the fury of white being kicked high into the air in towering plumes by invisible but violent currents.

I felt the slope before I could see it. The burn in my thighs and the increasing drag of my sledges alerted me to the fact that I was going uphill. The snow became firmer underfoot, packed down by the weight of the wind rushing over it. In places the snow had been scoured away completely to leave bald patches of ice which caught the light so that they gleamed a dirty grey. The SPOT tracks were gone, scoured away to leave no more than the occasional crosshatched imprint. It seemed implausible that just four days before, as I had flown overhead in a small ski plane gazing downwards, half a dozen tractors had hauled themselves over this very ground. Glancing directly upwards I could still see solid blue sky and the sun blazing unhindered by cloud, but all around me at ground level hazy squalls of wind-blown snow started to obscure my view. The drifts rose like sylphs from the ground, rushing towards me in gusts as if I was being attacked by wraiths. Occasionally I would catch sight of an indistinct mass of white darting towards me from the periphery of my goggle-restricted vision and it would make me physically jump in fright as if a vaporous mugger was about to tackle me to the ground.

Within hours the slope of the glacier became significantly steeper and I began breathing harder as I shortened my stride, feeling the weight of my sledges pulling me backwards. Despite the short strips of velvet-like material stuck to the underside of my skis to grip the snow, my footing frequently slipped on the increasingly icy surface and I concentrated on treading down hard to increase my hold. Waves of translucent white rolled towards me at intervals from the top of the glacier, the noise of the wind reaching a crescendo as it got closer, tearing at my clothing as it passed and momentarily obliterating my sight completely. Then it would be gone and I would look ahead for the next wave. I became very good at judging the speed of the oncoming surges, waiting until they were almost upon me before bowing my head into the airstream and adjusting my footing to brace myself against the force of the wind pushing against my body and sledges.

At first I tried to maintain my normal routine of moving for an hour or two before stopping for a short break to fill my mouth with chocolate and gulp some water but the increasing effort of pulling the sledges up an ever more slippery and steepening slope soon had me pausing every few minutes to lean on my ski poles and pull air into my lungs. During the pauses I glanced around me at the valley sides which now seemed very close. In places dark arêtes of exposed rock protruded from the white looking like the ribs of a shipwreck. The corridor of snow-covered ice was little more than a kilometre across and only the very peaks of the mountains were still visible on either side of me, buried almost to their tips by cracked and slumping layers of snow. It was hard not to imagine them as silent sentinels of stone looking down impassively at me, a tiny speck in a bright green jacket, inching along the central canal running between them.

Every pause lasted only a few moments but the interruption to my forward momentum made it more difficult each time to get started again. The muscles in my calves and thighs began to complain at the extra effort and my hips started to bruise with the pressure of the harness and the weight of the sledges. Taking miniature steps, it felt like I was barely moving and the lack of progress was frustrating. After each break I would set off with renewed determination, only to find that my body was soon begging for another pause. I had been going uphill all day and yet looking around me I judged I was only a third of the way up the slope I could see; I had no idea what lay beyond the horizon of my view. As I felt an internal anger build at my sluggish headway I suddenly heard my mother's voice, calm and clear in my head.

'Just keep going,' she said.

'Just keep moving forward.'

It was exactly the sort of practical advice my mother would produce in times of crisis and I found it reassuring. The important thing was that I was advancing, even if it was at a painfully slow rate. I repeated my mother's imagined advice over and over in rhythm with my measured steps, sometimes aloud and sometimes silently in my head:

'Keep moving forward.

Just keep moving forward.

Keep moving forward.'

The wind grew stronger as the glacier became steeper. The intervals between each wave of wind shortened until I was permanently immersed in a howling rage of air currents and snow. Regularly a particularly violent squall would hit me with such force that I would have to stop and brace myself with skis and poles, leaning forward into the wind to keep my balance. Several times a gust caught me off guard and I stumbled, my sledges sliding backwards over hard-won ground. Eventually, on the brink of losing my temper, I decided to take off my skis, hoping that walking would give me a better grip. I was aware that skis were my only defence against crevasses (by spreading my weight more evenly over the ground, wearing skis made it less likely that I would fall through any unseen snowbridges) but I couldn't bear the slipping and lurching any longer. I fastened the skis to the top of my sledge, taking care that there was no possibility of them working free and sliding all the way to the bottom of the glacier. Setting off again though, I was disappointed that the strength of the wind still made me stagger, even with the extra grip of my boot soles.

I thought about my tent. Pitching a tent in stormy conditions with a team was hard enough but now I would have to manage alone. The lightweight fabric seems to come alive in even the slightest of breezes, writhing like a tethered animal wanting to be free. It's both awkward and tiring to keep the tent pinned to the ground while placing poles and anchoring guy ropes. In preparation for the expedition I had thought hard about my solo pitching routine to try and lessen the risk of the tent blowing away during the process. I had even added a safety line so that I could clip the tent to my sledges or to myself until I was sure it was securely anchored. I drilled myself relentlessly so that the new routine became habit. One of my greatest fears was that in a moment of carelessness an unexpected gust of wind would snatch my tent away and I would be left without shelter, helpless against the perishing climate. But in the face of the winds that now surged around me, I was more worried that during the inevitable struggle with the tent my precious home would get damaged so badly that it would be useless. Without a tent my expedition would be over and I would be left exposed to the storm in a dangerous predicament.

I glanced around me at the narrow, steeply sloping glacier and realised for the first time that even in an emergency situation, it was highly unlikely a plane would be able to land anywhere near me and certainly not in these winds. I had seen the monumental logistical effort it had taken to get me to this 'wrong side' of Antarctica. I didn't imagine that a repeat performance of the flight across the continent from the basecamp at Union Glacier could be organised easily. With a heavy weight of dread in my stomach it became clear just how alone I truly was. Even if I used the satellite phone in my jacket pocket to call for an emergency evacuation, help would not be with me for a scarily long time. In the UK we have become used to the reassurance of Emergency Services and Search and Rescue teams, so that even when I have been alone in wilderness areas I have had the subconscious comfort of knowing that someone would be there to help me if I got into trouble. Now, I felt stripped of all safety nets. Whatever happened on this glacier, there would be nobody coming to rescue me, no one there to help. For the first time in my life I was completely and solely responsible for my own well-being.

'You have to get yourself out of this,' I told myself aloud.

The wind seemed to heighten its squalling right at that moment, slamming into my body with such force that I staggered backwards. My sledges became incredibly heavy as I pulled against both the slope and the wind resistance. The airborne snow had blotted out the horizon so that I couldn't tell how far I was from the top of the glacier but looking behind me I judged that I couldn't be more than half way. I felt a familiar fizz of adrenalin and fear crawl through my limbs. I grappled with my thoughts, trying to cling to anything objective and logical, but the temptation to give in to complete terror was too strong. Panic screamed through my mind like a beacon bleeping out an alert message over and over.

Simultaneously I noticed something different in the oncoming frenzy of white; a darker shade. I inched closer, breathing hard, my heart throbbing almost as loudly as the panic in my head. The shadow eventually revealed hard lines. It was manmade and I had seen its like before. In the middle of the glacier was a tall square wooden post surrounded by a cluster of green flags, identical to the LOO-JW post I had passed on my first day. I moved closer, fighting against the wind, and flung my arms around the sturdy anchor as soon as it was within reach. I could feel it vibrating, strummed by the wind. Leaning against it I could sense the strength of the wood. It would stand firm through any storm. With one arm hooked around the sturdy post I heaved at my sledges until they rested upslope of the marker, across the gradient of the glacier and safe from being blown downhill. I slumped on the sledges with my back to the wind trying to muster the energy to eat and drink.

I glanced at my watch. I would normally have planned to camp within the next hour or two. Peering uphill through the protective fur trim of my hood, I could see that the slope ahead looked even steeper and windier than the ground I had covered. What would happen if it simply got too windy to be able to pitch my tent? Did I have the energy to keep skiing until the wind dropped? I looked again at the post. At the top had been carved the code SPT-11 in a bold rounded font. I couldn't tell how deep the post had been struck into the ground but I was pretty sure it was the most solid anchor I was likely to find on the glacier. As another gust hit me so hard that I gripped hold of the sledges beneath me for balance, I made a decision.

I was going to pitch camp where I stood and tie my tent to the post.

I approached the task of pitching the Hilleberg like a general at war. Anything left unsecured would be blown away by the wind in an instant so I removed only one item from my sledge at a time, carefully re-fastening the sledge bags to prevent them being filled with drifting snow or anything being snatched by the blizzard. I moved slowly, staggering in the stronger gusts, firmly fixing the tent to the ground with my bodyweight as I rolled it out section by section, pinning down the unruly material with mounds of snow as I went.

Several times the wind caught the blade of my metal snowshovel like a sail, propelling it unpredictably towards me even though I clung on to its handle. In one gust it narrowly missed my face. I found it awkward to hold a shovel in one hand and control the tent with the other so I packed the shovel away and used my hands in generous bear-sized mitts to scoop up the snow around me. I had long, half-pipe snowpegs to anchor the guy ropes but they were no match for the winds tearing at the half-erected tent. The ground was too hard to drive in the end of my skis, so I chipped deep trenches for my skis and poles, looping the ends of the guy ropes around them before packing the trenches with snow so that it set as hard as stone on top of my improvised anchors.

The final guy rope I wrapped around the wooden post and secured with a carabiner which gave me hope that, even if my tent was flattened and destroyed by the wind, tying it to the post would at least stop me and the tent setting off down the glacier like a runaway bobsled. I did the same with my sledges, fastening them to the post and digging big pits so that they were buried up to their rims. Finally, retrieving my shovel, I laboriously heaped snow around the skirts of the tent so that by the time I had finished only the top half of the short tubular Hilleberg was still visible.

I stumbled around the perimeter of my shelter one last time, tensioning ropes and checking attachments before dropping to my knees and pushing myself through the constricted doorway. Hastily sealing the tent entrance behind me, I cowered on all fours in the small vestibule breathing hard. It had taken me two and a half hours to complete a task that usually took me no more than twenty minutes.

Shaking the worst of the snow from my clothing I pulled down my hood and ripped the mask and goggles from my face so that I could better look around me. The tent was being pummelled by regular waves of wind rolling down from the top of the glacier. With each hit the tent visibly flattened, putting immense strain on both the poles and the taut material. Despite the generous volume of snow piled on all sides to strengthen the structure, it looked as if my precious shelter might explode with the stress at any moment.

The noise was deafening, a mechanical roar that sent mind-numbing reverberations through the air. It was as thunderous as a cargo train passing just inches away but with the plangent reverberation of an earthquake. At first I thought the very ground I sat on was shaking; then I realised that it was me, trembling. I pulled a bear-paw mitt from one hand, holding my palm horizontally in the air close to my face and watched it quiver as affirmation. I felt frozen to the spot, unable to think or act. This time, unlike on my first evening, I recognised the sensation immediately. This was pure, instinctive, terror.

'Let the fear in,' my brain instructed, just as it had done before, and for the second time in my journey I sat in the snow, buried my head in my hands and sobbed.

I had never in my life felt so utterly beyond help, so reliant on my own initiative and yet so incapable. My mind lurched from one desperate scenario to the next: What if the tent split open and my belongings scattered across the glacier? What if the poles snapped and I was left trapped inside a flattened shelter? What if the tent was slowly shredded until it was useless, leaving me exposed and helpless?

As the tears subsided, so did the panic, and some semblance of the experienced explorer I was supposed to be took over. I pulled into the tent what was essential from my sledges and kept the equipment in a deep pit I dug in the entrance of my tent so that it wouldn't blow away if suddenly exposed to the wind. I made marks on the inside of the tent to show the levels of the snow shovelled around its sides so that I could monitor how quickly it was being scoured away and I made food, wriggling into my sleeping bag to eat in order to conserve the warmth it generated. Afterwards I lay wide-eyed on my back staring up at the roof which the squalls were beating and distorting like a blacksmith shaping steel. Occasionally a particularly violent gust would make me swear out loud in fright and I'd sit up looking everywhere at once, convinced that at any moment the tent would come apart. I wore everything but my jacket which I tucked securely underneath me in readiness for a sudden exposure to the elements.

Sleep was impossible. Even if I had been able to calm my frenzied mind, the noise and vibrations would have kept me awake. Every few hours I left the warmth of my sleeping bag, pulled on face mask, goggles, boots and jacket, zipping the jacket right up to my chin so that the fur trim of my hood formed a protective cocoon around my face, and pushed myself out of the tent into the maelstrom. Each time the force of the wind would take me by surprise and I'd stagger unsteadily. Occasionally I didn't bother standing up at all and shuffled around on my hands and knees, adding more snow to the heaps around the tent to replace any that had been blown away, tightening guy ropes and checking that the anchors I'd buried in the ground were still secure. The sun was high in the sky above the glacier on the southern reaches of its slow rotation, undaunted and undimmed by the weather below. Even in my desperate scrabbling in the snow and the terrifying fury of the winds, I couldn't resist pausing to look around me at the smoky squalls drifting gracefully beneath sun-kissed peaks. It seemed strange to be on the brink of calamity in such cheerful sunshine.

Back in the tent, I pulled my satellite phone out of my jacket pocket and discovered that in the struggle to pitch my tent I had snapped the aerial that extended from the top of the handset. The upper half of the receiver hung limply at an angle. The wires holding it together, normally hidden, were now clearly visible. I had a spare handset but changing my primary number would cause confusion that I would rather avoid, so I found the strong white tape that I use to prevent blisters and wrapped a length of it around the break. The aerial no longer retracted into the handset but when I pushed the power button the unit immediately leapt into life as normal. I felt relieved but also a little sad. The handset was a brand-new model lent to me by the manufacturers. It was so new that it wasn't even available to the public and yet now, just days into my trip, this piece of ultra-modern technology looked a little dejected, patched together with humble sticky tape.

I used the phone to send a message to the expedition Twitter account. This was a purely one-way form of communication, like sending a text message from a mobile phone. I couldn't receive any messages in reply or access the Internet; but somehow sharing news of my predicament seemed to lessen the oppressive awareness of being beyond ready help.

'Up every couple of hours to check on the tent,' I wrote.

'So not much sleep but proud of my little Hilleberg for surviving well.'

It was a far cry from what I wanted to write. I was desperate to share my worries but didn't want to descend into melodrama or cause unnecessary panic at home. I was mindful that my family were among those reading the messages. I sat with the satellite phone in my lap as if it was a magical device that could somehow create a more tangible link to my loved ones.

I remembered something my mother had first told me as a child but which had stuck with me ever since. I had been homesick on a school trip and she told me that if ever I felt far from home I should look at the moon and the stars and remember that she would be looking at the same moon, the same stars and the same night sky. Many times the thought had brought comfort. It made me feel closer to my family even when, eventually, my travels took me so far that the night sky I gazed at was no longer the same as that which sparkled over my parents. As I lay in my sleeping bag, feeling the vibrations of my battered tent, there was no darkness at all, no moon or stars to console me, but the sentiment remained. I knew my family were thinking of me, that they trusted me to get myself home safely. I've always been aware that part of the reason I have been able to travel so far and for so long is because I've felt the strength of that trust.

I regularly get asked about my parents, as if my desire to explore can be explained in some way by my upbringing or that it is perhaps due to a quirk in my DNA inherited from the genes of adventurous ancestors. My parents were adventurous for their time although their travels would probably be considered rather tame by today's standards of exotic backpacking. While I was still a baby they drove through Greece and Italy exploring sleepy islands and discovering quiet villages. I learnt to walk in the dust of southern Italy and first swam in the shallows of the Greek coast. Perhaps these early adventures were responsible for a nascent wanderlust but I don't have any memories of my own of those days. The travels I do remember as a child were mostly modest family holidays involving a camper van and a soggy corner of England. Once or twice we were treated to a package holiday in a reliably sunny part of Europe, in resorts with synthetic blue pools and all-you-can-eat buffets as divorced from the local culture as the fenced hotel complexes we stayed in. And yet, our family never really seemed to fit comfortably into this ready-made mould of organised tours and hotel activities. I remember a delicious feeling of rebellion at abandoning tightly choreographed coach trips to do our own exploring, delighting in the fact that we were always the last family back on board, our arms full of exciting local produce that we had haggled for ourselves.

My parents were never afraid of plunging into the relatively unknown and trying something new and this was most evident not in travel but in the kitchen. The shelves at home were always stacked with spices and exotic ingredients that they or their friends had brought back from far-flung places. I was the only child I knew who was regularly presented with tagines, samosas or dolmades for tea. I didn't always welcome the unfamiliar cuisine at the time but now I recognise that the enthusiasm of my Mum and Dad instilled in me a curiosity for difference and the confidence to be open to new cultures when I was eventually old enough to experiment for myself.

However, there is a part of my desire for adventure that I can't attribute to parental influence. Much of it is simply an integral part of who I am, as tangible and intrinsic as my height or the colour of my eyes. From the start I couldn't help but see the possibility for adventure wherever I happened to be. Growing up surrounded by woodland I saw the trees and fields as potential locations for secret camps or homemade zip-wires. Mum has a photo of me aged seven or eight sitting under a bedsheet thrown over a string I'd tied between the trunks of two closely spaced trees. I'm trying (unsuccessfully) to toast marshmallows over a miserable smouldering of twigs which I no doubt imagined to be a most excellent camp fire. My sister has been dragged along to be my tent-mate and we are both grinning, bursting with pride at the success of our big expedition even though we are barely out of sight of our own front door.

As a fully grown woman I was still messing about in tents but hunkered down on a windswept glacier, it didn't feel like fun anymore. In between snatching fits of sleep and plunging outside for bouts of vigorous digging I resolved my next move. It was tempting just to sit tight in my tent and hope for the winds to lessen but having watched the currents of snow swirling from the crest of the glacier I was more convinced than ever that these were katabatic winds that could be capable of keeping up their terrifying intensity for days. My tent had withstood the pounding so far but each time it was struck by another fierce gust I winced in expectation of catastrophe. If anything, the storm seemed to be gaining strength. I drank my breakfast coffee slowly, watching wisps of steam from my mug deform into jagged zigzags as the movement of the tent fabric in the squalls pulled the pocket of air within from side to side. I could feel the sluggish weariness of a disturbed night behind my eyes but I wanted to be gone, I was desperate to escape this place.

Reversing my technique of the previous evening, I dismantled my camp one arduous step at a time, taking care to keep the flighty tent under tense control. It was almost three hours before I finally straightened up over two securely packed sledges, my tent firmly lashed to the top in a tight cigar-shaped roll around the tent poles which were still in place within the folds of material. Having dug my skis out of their temporary graves I stowed them in my sledges, deciding to continue in my boots with a ski pole in each hand. Before I set off I paused to rest my fist on the thrumming wooden post as a gesture of appreciation. SPT-11 had been my only glimmer of security and I was grateful for its solid comfort.

The wind tore at my jacket as if invisible fingers were plucking at me. I felt encircled by a rage I couldn't see. Even in my boots I had to lean heavily on my ski poles, their spikes gaining a precarious purchase on the icy surface. I kept my head bowed, watching my feet making tiny, jerky steps as if climbing miniature stairs. The rhythm of step and ski pole as I moved forward was remorseless – tap, tap, tap – refusing to submit to my rasping breathing, the aches in my calves or the dull throb of the sledge weight around my hips and lower back. It was a mechanical effort and I felt strangely disembodied from the process; I was being propelled by muscle and bone, the fundamental engineering of my body, and it appeared to have little to do with what thoughts passed through my brain. All thinking seemed to stop, replaced with a dispassionate register of pattern and tempo. When I did eventually look up I could see the lip of the glacier above me still and snow being flung from its summit like water frothing over a waterfall. I felt my heartbeat quicken. This was undoubtedly the steepest and windiest section. I pushed on before I had time to be intimidated. I wondered how I would have felt if I had continued the previous day and met this vortex. I concentrated on the rhythm and thought about the words on the locket from my sister, 'Every step'.

I quickly lost track of time, pushing on when I should have paused for breaks, pulling against gust after gust, staggering and slipping but refusing to allow myself to stop. I was so utterly fixated on each step that I'm not sure when exactly I first noticed the onslaught of waves begin to slow, or the intensity of each gust diminishing. I just remember looking up and finding myself in the centre of a flat bottomed bowl, sheltered on all sides by gentle banks of snow. And I remember the quiet. My ears rang with the absence of that roaring, rushing wind.

It was over.

I dropped to my knees and cried, releasing all the stress and anxiety of the previous night. I ripped off my goggles and face mask and, still crying, fished the GPS from my pocket. I waited, snivelling, as the unit searched for satellites. Then it told me that I had travelled just three nautical miles from my last camp. I roared in frustration. If I had followed my instinct and kept skiing the day before rather than camping on the windiest stretch of the glacier I would have reached this sheltered bowl and saved myself a whole evening of exhausting heartache – not to mention the hours I had lost pitching and striking my tent in such difficult conditions. I wanted to weep at the waste of it all but right then I was too angry to cry.

I sat on my sledge and relaxed a little into the stillness. There was a sense of physical relief as if stretching my legs after a long-haul flight. I used the opportunity to go to the loo without worrying about being blown over and to sort out my layers of clothing that had been hastily thrown on in the eagerness to strike camp that morning. Feeling a lot more comfortable I put on my skis and set off across the bowl. I could see a steep bank at the far end and sure enough, as I reached the top I re-emerged into the path of the wind but it was nothing like as strong as it had been before. It had lost its rage, like an irascible old man who loses the thread of his argument. Instead the ferocity transferred to the battle raging inside my own head. On the one hand I was furious with myself for not following my instinct and attempting to ski through the worst of the winds but at the same time I found solace in the thought that there was no way I could have known. Those I had spoken to about the glacier hadn't mentioned the bowl at the top, probably because it was so hard to detect from a vehicle, and it was certainly not as significant to them in a truck as it was to me on skis. If the next person to ski up the Leverett Glacier asked my advice I would be able to warn them not to make the same mistake.

I consoled myself with the realisation that 'not knowing' is supposed to be part of the excitement of being first, the reward of priority. When Scott, Shackleton and Amundsen searched for a route through this very same chain of mountains a century before they had even less information about what they might find. Antarctica was still a place of fantastical possibility and conjecture. At the time, the scientific expectation that they would find an inland sea at the South Pole was so plausible that they could have been forgiven for carrying boats with them. Another, perhaps less revered theory, predicted that they would find a gateway to the hollow centre of the Earth. From our modern perspective of knowledge it is easy to forget what to be 'unknown' truly means. As I skied away from the top of the Leverett Glacier, petulantly reproaching myself for a decision that was made for good reason but ultimately flawed, it was perhaps the closest I would ever come to experiencing, in some small way, a taste of the frustrations and dilemmas that those early pioneers must have faced on a daily basis.

I managed another two miles before camping on the top of an escarpment overlooking the gap in the mountains I had climbed through. To cover only five nautical miles in a day was demoralising but I had gained a lot of height. I seemed to be level with the very tops of the mountains that had towered over me just the day before. Still, the experience on the glacier had left me shaken. Even though there was now only enough wind to send long streams of snow drifting along the ground, I spent much longer than necessary creating deep and secure anchors, burying my skis in cavernous trenches to hold the guy ropes and entombing the tent in a deluge of shovelled snow. Crawling wearily into the shelter of my little Hilleberg I realised that being inside the tent now felt like a sanctuary rather than a confinement. The past twenty-four hours had bonded us. I fussily arranged my kit along the walls of the sleeping compartment and felt both grateful and reassured by its protection. The Hilleberg was my home on the ice and for the first time I saw it as cosy. The subdued yellow light of the tent and the reassuring roar of my stove cheerfully providing both warmth and water were to become the two most important blessings within my Antarctic home.

CHAPTER FOUR

FORTY-SIX

@felicity_aston Yesterday was the first day I didn't burst into tears at any point. Must mean I'm getting used to this finally?

Imagine lying in the sun on a summer's day looking up at an unobscured view of a cloudless sky. Staring up into the blue, nothing is visible except a single uniform colour. There is no structure to focus on, no variation in shade or texture, no sense of distance, dimension or scale. And yet, in time, barely perceptible shapes seem to appear, sometimes as constantly shifting patterns of light and dark. Eventually, it seems, the sky is not uniform after all but filled with forms that are almost familiar yet hover just beyond recognition. Scientists call this a Ganzfeld, a homogeneous visual field, and our reaction to it highlights the inability of our brains to accept the concept of 'nothing'. Normally the brain harvests the visual stimulus around us and converts it into what we 'see'. When that data disappears the brain fills in the blanks, creating the vaguest impression of a world that isn't there. It creates forms and shapes that are almost recognisable because they are drawn from a melding of our memories and experience of sight over a lifetime.

For decades parapsychologists looking for evidence of psychic abilities, telepathy and extrasensory perception have created artificial Ganzfelds. Subjects are often blindfolded, placed in enclosed rooms flooded with red light, their hearing restricted to only white noise and static. Some are confined to special beds or inside flotation tanks to produce almost total sensory deprivation. The research into parapsychology has so far proved inconclusive but the dramatic effect of a Ganzfeld on the brain isn't disputed. The electrical activity of the brain changes and it often produces nearly immediate hallucinations that can be both vivid and complex.

A polar whiteout has to be one of the most perfect natural Ganzfelds imaginable.

It had been a week since I had struggled to the top of the Leverett Glacier and the weather I had enjoyed beneath the Transantarctic Mountains was now nothing but a distant memory. For the last seven days cloud had blotted out the blue so thickly and with such tenacity that it was hard to imagine that the sky had ever been anything other than the palest of greys. The weather descended to the ground, eclipsing any peripheral view and cloaking me in a cocoon of gritty white. As I skied through the gloom I could sense rather than see the huge masses of cloud drifting around me like stealthy battleships. The silence that had suffocated me during my first few days on the ice was replaced by a continuous white noise of blizzard and storm. The wind threw snow into the air, further reducing the light that was already diminished to the dullness of dusk by the dense murk. There wasn't enough light to create even the most ghostly of shadows and the absence of contrast made everything appear unnaturally flat. The ridges and hollows, the furrows and folds that usually gave the snow underfoot its texture had all vanished as if a delicate pencil drawing had been recklessly erased to leave just the grubby white paper beneath. The world was reduced to a single dimension: flat, homogenous, grey. It was a flawless Antarctic Ganzfeld.

Every now and then as I skied staring forward into the void ahead I'd feel a sense of complete unreality that would make my head spin. I'd feel dizzy, my eyes unable to fix on a single solid point of reference and I'd be struck by the peculiar sensation that I was falling. It was like an extreme form of vertigo. Each time it happened I'd stop to turn and look at my two sledges which still sat reassuringly on the ground beneath them. Without a horizon they were the only clue as to the division between snow and sky. My brain would need a few moments to re-orientate itself, and I'd wait while it gripped hold of the sledges as the only available fixed point in space, until the dizzy spinning eventually stopped.

I quickly realised that I couldn't rely on my own senses in these surreal surroundings. All perspective was lost. In a world where the normal rules of physics didn't seem to apply anymore I felt strangely vulnerable and the spongy diaphanous mass surrounding me began to assume an eeriness that I couldn't shake off. A ghostly black blob appeared in the miasma and swam around in space randomly. Having given up trying to work out what it was and resorting instead to ignoring it completely, I almost skied right over it. The blob was a flag marking the SPOT route. It had been firmly fixed on the ground the whole time and yet, to me, it had appeared to dart about like a UFO. My judgement of scale and distance was confused by the fact that the terrain hadn't flattened out after passing through the narrows of the Leverett Glacier but continued irregularly upward over a series of hills. The UFO flag that had appeared to float above me was probably simply at the top of a hill and it had moved around as I had gained or lost height.

The wind never stopped, continuously circulating in currents and flows, its gusts and eddies always searching and probing for some weakness, be it the slightest of gaps between my face mask and goggles or some item of equipment stowed on my sledge that was in danger of being pulled free. The winds left a thick layer of soft snow on the ground so that my skis sank a full three or four inches into the surface with every stride, slowing further my already sluggish movement up inclines that felt endless because I was unable to see the top in the bad visibility. The only reason I knew I was climbing at all was because my sledges would suddenly feel much heavier and my pace slowed as I began to breathe harder. The lack of progress despite such backbreaking effort was demoralising. On one particularly bad day I made less than three nautical miles in over ten hours of dogged skiing.

The time lost on the Leverett Glacier and now the relentless, slow slogs uphill in soft snow and bad weather weighed heavily on my mind. Each evening I marked my location on the map and made increasingly desperate calculations in my tiny notepad, searching for some consolation in the numbers – but there was none to be had. Whichever way I looked at it, there was no possibility that in these conditions I was going to be able to make up the time and mileage I had lost. I tried not to let myself get despondent but the terrain, the loneliness, the unexpected delays, the unyielding weather and the sheer effort of each day took its toll. Every night as I lay in my sleeping bag waiting for sleep I would listen to the menacing echo of the air's restlessness, magnified by the crack and rumble of tent fabric. I imagined each surge that blasted my shelter to be a breaker in a vast ocean. The wind of the South, like the waves of the ocean, gain their power over a fetch of a thousand miles and in my mind's eye the tent became a small boat tossed in the swell, the agitated material around me transformed into the clatter of badly trimmed sails and the dry snow being blown against my tent sounding uncannily like the spray of the sea. I lingered on the thought that my presence was as inconsequential to the wind of Antarctica as flotsam to the waves of the Atlantic.

I had prayed for a calm day but the first thing I heard when I woke was the continued thunder of wind and the brittle report of the tent convulsing around me. Still in my sleeping bag I unzipped a chink in the tent door and looked out into solid white. As I peered outward looking for any hint of a horizon, puffs of drifting snow exploded through my tiny peephole spraying the hood of my sleeping bag with ice crystals that promptly melted into tiny pools. I closed the gap and lay back into the warmth of my down bag. Staring upwards at the chequered weave of the tent a few feet above my face, my mind digested the fact that the day ahead would be as hard as the day that had just passed. I was filled with a deadening conviction; I couldn't go on.

Antarctica was more than I could manage on my own. I could not get out of the tent and confront the remorseless weather that waited for me. I could not spend another day inching forward on my skis trying to ignore the clammy discomfort of the close-fitting material around my face. I could not bear anymore the moment I would be forced to expose myself to the cold, hastily refastening stubborn clothing with painfully numbing fingers, only to repeat the agonising process a few hours later. I couldn't countenance another day cramming tasteless half-frozen food into jaws that ached with the repeated exertion of chewing such toughness. The relentless struggle just to stay safe, never mind move forward, was more than I could take. I understood now, categorically, that the distance ahead of me and the number of days to come, as well as my alone-ness, was more, much more, than I could face. It wasn't that I was giving in; it was a calm and rational realisation that I didn't have the physical or mental capacity for the challenge ahead. I had found what I had come for. I had found my limit. All that remained was for me to decide how I was to get home. As this knowledge sank in I didn't feel regret that my journey was over, only slight surprise that I had reached the end so soon.

Revelling in the feeling of relief and release that came with the thought that I didn't have to leave my sleeping bag or the safety of my flimsy shelter, I planned when to make the phone call to Union Glacier informing them of my decision. Absorbed by the practicalities, I didn't at first notice a growing sensation welling in another part of my mind. The sensation wasn't yet a conscious thought; but it would slowly reveal itself to be the knowledge that I couldn't give up but had to find the determination to continue. As soon as this thought made itself heard, my mind was torn by a war of wills, split between the complete resolve not to go on and the simultaneous understanding that I didn't have any choice but to keep going.

Reassuring both halves of my battling brain that it was neither a sign of staying or leaving, I crawled out of my sleeping bag and started the habitual chores of my morning routine. Distracted by the emotional chaos within, I moved mechanically around the tent pulling on clothes, scraping off the ice that accumulated on the inside of the vestibule, priming then lighting the stove and watching the small flame grow into the blue-blaze of full flare.

I ran my gaze repeatedly over the slogan that I had spontaneously scrawled above the tent door in black marker while still in the basecamp at Union Glacier, 'Let routine take command of feeling'. It was a phrase I had read in Erling Kagge's book about becoming the first person to ski solo to the South Pole, and it perfectly distilled something I had already experienced myself; that strict routines often provide a momentum that can overcome any emotional reluctance. I recited the phrase under my breath as if it had some magical power. I willed myself to focus only on my routine, to deaden my emotional response in order to rationally evaluate my ability to continue. Then the noise of the wind outside brought with it a sudden memory of skiing through the benumbing nothingness, stumbling through an invisible landscape, the acrid sting of the cold, the monotonous repetition of hour after hour. All my careful objectivity would be eroded, drawing the emotion to the surface once again like magma being drawn through the Earth's crust before a volcanic eruption. The internal turmoil became so intense that the emotion spilled over and I burst into tears, sobbing pathetically as I made my breakfast coffee. To an observer it would have appeared that I had lost my mind. Even to me it felt like the onset of a peculiar kind of madness.

Despite the fact that I felt complete inertia in every molecule of my being it was clear that somehow I had to move forward, I had no choice but to get myself out of the tent – but knowing is only the first part of doing. Having reached the end of my morning routine I sat in the vestibule of the tent, fully dressed for a day in the open, my belongings properly packed in bags by the still tightly zipped doorway. All that remained was to step outside but still I hesitated, lingering over the last mouthfuls of coffee in my heavily insulated mug, listening fearfully to the wind. I glared at the words above the door until they lost all meaning and became nothing but a series of uneven strokes and scratches, empty hieroglyphics. My mind scrabbled for a mental prop, a cerebral foothold that would enable me to propel myself out of the door. I tried to coax myself the way I would a child, with promises of an extra coffee at the end of the day, an additional five minutes in the warmth of my sleeping bag the next morning or a luxurious rest day of sleep and comfort tomorrow (a promise I knew even then to be improbable).

When that failed, I took a more prosaic approach, forcing myself to think of all the sponsors I would be letting down if I refused to move, of all those people who had written encouraging emails before I left, people I knew would be following my progress eagerly every day. How could I disappoint them? I tried to shame myself into action by imagining that I was being filmed and that my reluctance would be broadcast over the Internet to all those who believed I was made of more resilient stuff than this.

However, the greatest source of motivation turned out not to be those who had supported me. It seems contrary, when I have been very fortunate to receive generous encouragement from many wonderful people, but in fact it was the exact opposite. It was by remembering those who had been disparaging of me in the past, or events that had left me feeling angry and indignant, that provided the greatest incentive. I needed to prove people wrong or, rather, to prove to myself that those people were wrong. I recalled those who had dismissed me, people who had been unjustly harsh in their evaluation of my character and my capability, in order to galvanise myself. Perhaps it is natural that the strongest feelings provoke the most dramatic responses. Hurt so often stays with us longer and more vividly than praise.

Sitting in the entrance of the tent I revived ancient wounds. I thought about the trusted team-mate who unfairly attributed to me every set-back of the expedition we shared, later summarising in a report to our peers that I 'lacked mental toughness'. I resented anew the remarks of an experienced polar explorer and personal hero that I had been thrilled and honoured to meet who commented that the expeditions I had toiled through and fought for were 'just a bit of fun for the girls'.

Most of all I dwelled on my time at Rothera with the British Antarctic Survey. I remembered the smart of the disapproval I'd sensed from a handful of colleagues who felt that my attitude was wrong, that I wasn't appreciative enough of my surroundings and therefore didn't deserve to be there at all. I don't know if it was because, at the age of twenty-three, I was the youngest on base, or because I enjoyed the parties and pop-up bars on station as much as the landscape outside, but for whatever reason they wrote me off as unworthy, denying me the opportunity for responsibility whenever they could and refusing to see that I had anything to offer. For someone who had always been a high achiever this was a bitter injustice. In many ways the frustration of that experience had driven me ever since. It's not that I seek the approval of those who have underestimated me. It is entirely for my own benefit that I want to have tangible proof of what I already know: that they were wrong about me; that I have the potential to be more.

The anger, resentment and frustration revived by these recollections were the kick I needed. Like a ratchet slipping into the teeth of a cog, the decision was made and there was no going back. I sighed deeply, tugged at the zips of the tent door and pulled myself out into the white.

My sense of purpose was restored but I knew it was only a temporary reprieve. The mental anguish of the last few hours had not been unique. I'd had the same conviction every single morning since leaving the Leverett. Every time I woke, the first thought on opening my eyes had been the same: I could not get out of the tent and face another day. I went through the same internal dialogue morning after morning but the strength of my determination to quit and subsequent determination to persevere never diminished. It was a mental angst that I began to dread before I closed my eyes at night, knowing what waited for me when I woke. I realised, even in that first fortnight, that the success or failure of my expedition was not going to be determined by blizzards, crevasses, extreme cold or technical skill. It was going to depend purely and simply on whether or not I had the ability to get out of the tent each and every morning. That was the true challenge of this expedition. It sounds so simple and yet this physically undemanding act became one of the hardest tasks I had ever faced.

Perhaps in light of this, it was inevitable that one morning I would fail.

Although I had travelled nearly 200 kilometres from my start point I was still not clear of the brutal weather that broiled around the mountains. A few times during the previous week of bad weather the clouds had parted briefly to allow a glimpse of the world beyond, like looking through a wormhole to an alternative universe. I was allowed ephemeral views to my left of the snow sloping away in undulations, ending abruptly like the lip of an unseen waterfall as it met the heavily ice-covered peaks of the Transantarctic Mountains. Now that I had climbed way above 2,000 metres only the very tops of the mountains were visible over the horizon, as if I was walking on a level with their summits, but I was a little disappointed that they appeared to be so close. It was a reminder of how little progress I had made and of how far I still had to go.

There was another reason to be uneasy at the proximity of the mountains. One brief clearing in the clag of cloud revealed the ground nearest to me. My eyes widened in alarm as I picked out broad parallel indentations in the smooth snow over slopes to my left – the zebra-stripes of crevassed ground. It was difficult to judge size and distance but they could have been as little as a kilometre away. Seeing such fractured terrain so close made my skin crawl with anxiety. As the view was slowly obliterated by the cloud and I was once again cocooned in oppressive gloom I was effectively blind. With my only protection against crevasses being my own vigilance I felt frighteningly vulnerable. It suddenly seemed extremely foolish to be blundering across this landscape in such bad visibility before I'd reached the relative safety of the plateau where the ice is more solid and crevasses are less common. My nerves slowed my pace and my eyes ached with the strain of glaring at the snow in front of my ski tips for any sign of crevasses. I decided that if I could still see some evidence of my own tracks in the snow behind me, I had at least some chance of noticing any unusual slumps in the ground ahead that might betray the presence of a crevasse before I stepped on it. It was a flimsy safety margin however you looked at it but at least it gave me some kind of framework to cling to. I decided to camp when I noticed my ski tracks vanished behind me as swiftly as the wake of a ship on the ocean, blown away by the wind as a foam trail is dissolved by water.

Stepping out of the tent the next morning, the habitual debate raged to and fro in my head. I peered into the gloom. It felt good to be upright. I stretched my back and let the wind buffet me on the spot, leaning into the support of the gusts. Behind me my tent looked as if it was floating. It resembled a Photoshop image on a white screen waiting to be superimposed onto a landscape. My eyes swam with the lack of perspective, my brain struggling to make sense of the absence of everything. I walked a short distance from the tent but on turning found that my footprints left not the barest trace, obscured immediately by the spindrift racing across the snow at ground level. As I considered my options, snow began to fill the air so that even my tent – just a dozen feet from me – started to look faded, its edges blurred like a grainy photograph. In such weather I could step into the Grand Canyon without spotting it first, so my chances of detecting the delicate signs of crevassing I'd seen nearby the previous day were minimal. The day fell short of every safety margin I had given myself so I went back to the tent and decided not to move.

My decision was grounded in good sense but in retrospect it is clear to me that the previous week of battling into foul weather and soft snow with heavy sledges probably contributed a greater part to my reasoning. I got out of the tent several times throughout the day to assess the weather but I don't think that, if I was honest with myself, I had any real intention of moving. Instead I sat inside the tent agonising over my decision and compensating for it by thinking up as many good uses for my time as possible. I heaved my second sledge into the vestibule of my tent so that I could reorganise my daily ration bags and consolidate all the food I hadn't eaten. Despite the fact that I still felt nauseous most of the time I was at least now managing to eat a full meal every evening and a good portion of the chocolate and snacks allocated during the day.

I made some small adjustments to my kit and then turned my attention to a problem I had been steadfastly ignoring for a while. At some point during my battle up the Leverett Glacier I had noticed that the heel of my right foot was rolling off the shaft of my ski with every step. The boots I wore were of a traditional design, a soft wool boot encased in an outer layer of stiffened canvas and leather, and were attached by a clamp-like binding at the toe leaving the heel free to make a walking motion easier on the cross-country skis. The constant slip was causing an ache across the top of my foot and up into my shin. To prevent the ache turning into an injury I could feel myself compensating with each stride and this in turn was putting pressure on my already temperamental knee. It was clear that the binding had been fastened to the ski off-centre by an infinitesimal amount, even though by sight it looked perfectly straight. I hadn't noticed the problem during my short training weekends before departure and it was only now, a fortnight into the expedition, that the problem became apparent.

It was awkward to manoeuvre a 194 cm ski around a small two-person tent but I warmed the ski first next to my body before later suspending it over the explosive heat of my palm-sized stove. I waited until both the ski and the metal binding were hot to the touch before heaving at the screws with my penknife. I made no impact whatsoever and the screws remained tightly in position. The binding had been attached in a workshop so that there was no chance of it working loose – this made it impossible for me to adjust it in the tent with only my penknife. I had already tried placing my boot in the binding at an angle so that my foot sat straight on the ski but the boot always worked loose and the constant stopping to adjust it was worse than the original fault. I resigned myself to the fact that I would have to ski with an awkward gait. I hoped the effect on my knee wouldn't be catastrophic but when I thought of the hundreds of kilometres still ahead of me it seemed impossible that the situation could end in anything but calamity. I mentally castigated myself for bringing new and therefore untested skis. The thought of my old but trusty pair sitting at home made me want to weep. They had already seen me safe and comfortable to the Pole on one occasion and would doubtless have done so again.

Running out of jobs, I allowed myself time to snooze indulgently, savouring the sybaritic sense of security and protection from the weather outside, lounging in the delicious warmth and plumpness of my down bag, soaking up the comforting yellow glow of the tent as if it were sunlight. As I relaxed, an idea drifted to the front of my mind. I had only one set of clothes which I wore constantly, regardless of whether I was sleeping or skiing. There was never usually a reason to ever take them off but, with time on my hands, I decided to attempt some laundry. I melted a little extra snow and poured it into an empty ration bag. The bag wasn't big enough to tackle anything larger than a pair of knickers but I considered that underwear was probably a priority after two weeks of travel. I swished my underwear around in the bag of hot water, doing my best to recreate the spin motion of a washing machine, stopping when I judged they were clean. I wrang out the flimsy material before hanging them up over an elastic line on the sunny side of the tent vestibule feeling very pleased with my afternoon's work.

I was less smug when I checked on my drying laundry a few hours later. Although at first glance they seemed to be airing nicely I soon realised that they had actually frozen solid. When I lifted them off the line they remained bent in half and were so stiff that they could stand freely on the floor of the tent like a bizarre modernist sculpture. All that had been achieved by the drip dry was a row of short stubby icicles hanging from the gusset. I chipped off as much of the ice from the material as I could before placing the frozen knickers back in the sun, unsure what else I could do. The fate of my underwear was in the hands of Antarctica and cold temperature physics.

The next day was as gloomy and windswept as the last and even though the devil on my shoulder whispered alluringly that I would be perfectly justified in waiting another day, that the weather was clearly too bad for travel, that I still had little hope of seeing any crevasses, I reluctantly ignored it. The weather had been more or less unchanging for more than a week and from what I knew of Antarctic weather, it was more than likely to continue for days. I couldn't afford to hide in my tent indefinitely. Emboldened by a day's rest I made the decision to move on. Concentrating on the practical details of my preparations for the day ahead, I was careful not to let myself dwell on thoughts of the weather, the cold, or the distance remaining to the Pole. I focused instead on the level of fuel in the stove, the positioning of the mask around my face, the packing of my few bags and the placing of the satellite phone in my jacket pocket out of harm's way. Finding my underwear still stubbornly frozen on the line, I securely attached it to the outside of my sledge bag in the hope that perhaps it would freeze-dry in the wind.

Barely two hours after first opening my eyes I was on my way, head bowed into the wind, eyes fixed on the tips of my skis ploughing into monotonous white. Flapping wildly in the wind from the very back of the trailing sledge, like a proudly displayed ensign towed ingloriously across Antarctica, flew my frozen knickers.

My determination not to spend another day in the tent was rewarded by the appearance of the sun late in the day. It was an occurrence that had been so rare since I'd left the Ross Ice Shelf that at first I wasn't sure what it was. I marvelled at the great pools of silver that appeared on the landscape, spots of such brilliance that they made the rest of the scene look like scuffed steel. The spotlights of sunshine prising their way through the cloud cover never reached me but the variety of shade and colour at least fixed the position of the ground and gave a hint of a horizon to aim for. The light wasn't bright enough to create shadow and texture but it banished some of the gloom and the eeriness. Now, instead of appearing ghostly, the grey looked soft and soothing, everything blending gently into an elegant smoothness. Patches of ice gathered the weak light and reflected a pale luminous blue. My skis hit the ice with a rasp but, noticing that the weight of my sledges seemed to disappear as they trailed over the blue patches, I began to aim for them, grateful for the brief respite from the tugging at my hips. The icy patches enlarged and linked together until I found myself able to glide almost exclusively on the shiny pools, never touching snow. I felt like I was skating rather than skiing. By the end of the day I had covered almost fifteen nautical miles. My grin was so wide when the figure appeared on my GPS that it cracked the skin of my lips. A spell had been broken. I was sure that things were going to get better.

The voices of reluctance in my head were still as strong the following morning but I found it just a little easier to ignore them. The moment I emerged from the arched entrance of the Hilleberg into the acerbic wind I felt almost glad to be in the open. The old sense of euphoria crept through me and although in the bad visibility I couldn't tell if my sight stretched a thousand miles or a few feet, it seemed as if my spirit soared to fill the space I could sense around me.

My tent had been deluged by windblown snow while I had slept. The white loess filled every hollow, repairing all the imperfections left by my footprints and ski tracks, and formed graceful sloping drifts against the sides of my little green shelter. A ridge, grown almost as tall as the tent, trailed downwind. The particles of snow, so delicate when they fell, had coalesced to form a solid mass as dense as soil. I stumbled around the perimeter with my shovel, the dim light making it difficult to see the heaps of snow even though they were at least two foot high. I sank to my knees to dig and became submerged in the spindrift being blown along the surface in a thick layer. It was like sinking into a white river. Protected within my layers of fleece and windproof membrane, with the fur-edged hood of my jacket pulled close in a tight circle around my face, peering out through cheerfully tinted goggles

I felt removed from the weather as if safely ensconced in my own private submarine bubble. Today the cold didn't seem to penetrate my layers as it had done and as I bowed into the spray, breaking vigorously into the snow encasing my tent, I felt electrically alive. I was living the kind of adventure that had enthralled my imagination as a child. As unlikely as it was for the teenager who had avoided sport at all costs and the woman who disliked gyms, here I was, a real-life explorer. I couldn't help but feel thrilled with my own good fortune. Even though it was cold and miserable and lonely, I couldn't deny that the adventurer in me was perversely savouring every minute of it.

The drifting snow had obliterated all the patches of ice that had delighted me the day before but the light continued to get brighter as I travelled. I even noticed a few slivers of blue in the grey caul above me. On the ground I could make out vague structures like wavelets on a lake made solid. Occasionally a wavelet would rise out of the frozen surface higher than the others and curl over at its windward end. The inside of the curl was always a powder blue that showed up against the dull white like a pale eye and soon I began to notice these unwinking blue eyes dotting the ground ahead of me. They became larger and then appeared clustered together in groups, betraying large formations of wind-gouged snow that despite being up to a metre high and several metres long would be largely invisible until I was almost upon them. These wind-sculpted structures are known by their Russian name, sastrugi, and I was expecting them. Despite the fact that sastrugi are constantly shifting like sand dunes in the desert, ceaselessly changing the surface of Antarctica so that no place ever looks the same from year to year, it seems that the largest and most dense sastrugi always occur in the eighty-seventh degree of latitude, forming a loose band around the Pole like an asteroid belt around the sun. The Americans call it 'Sastrugi National Park' and with satisfaction I noted it meant I had completed my first full degree of latitude since leaving the coast. It was a tenuous milestone to celebrate but I grasped hold of it regardless and enjoyed the thought that I was skiing into a brand new degree.

After skiing for just over ten hours I stopped to camp in a tight space between two large configurations of sastrugi, each motionless wave curling over the last like a pod of porpoising dolphins trying to outdo each other. Once I had finished pitching the tent and pushed all the items I would need from my sledges into the vestibule, I lingered outside in the open to appreciate my unusually scenic campsite. The sun was burning a circular impression in the white sky above. A solar halo surrounded it, the lower edge of the silver ring almost brushing the grey suggestion of a horizon. It was mournfully beautiful and felt like a benediction from the heavens. I took it as a sign of protection and encouragement.

I woke several times during the night to feel the blaze of sunshine on my face through the thin fabric of the tent. The weather had turned. I felt as excited as a child on Christmas morning as I abandoned my strict morning routine, throwing on my clothes before breakfast so that I could scramble out of the tent to take a look. If I hadn't been so stiff from lying on the ground I would have jumped for joy. Instead I made my cheeks hurt with the width of my grin and I felt myself whimper pathetically, hovering between laughter and tears. The sky was blue. A pale opaline blue, but blue nonetheless. It wasn't a perfect day but the sky was back and the clouds had reduced to translucent towers of vapour drifting overhead.

Despite the flood of drifting snow that made everything a little bleary, I could see a clear horizon and a panoply of texture had rematerialised on the ground. The sastrugi were now revealed in every detail. As I turned on the spot devouring the view I suddenly realised what was missing. I span my head around the horizon to be sure. It was true. The mountains were gone. I felt a slight sense of shock; they had been so close just a few days before but now there was not so much as a blip on the skyline to betray that they had ever existed. It meant that I was well and truly on the polar plateau. The next feature I would see would be the Thiel Mountains some 800 kilometres away. Until then, the level, unremitting horizon would be my only geography.

As if trying to compensate for the lack of larger scale topography, the sastrugi grew in size and number during the day. Sleek lines of graceful arcs and domes rose out of the ground, sculpted by the wind into fantastical shapes. I passed rolling horses and waiting toads, predatory fish and majestic orcas, sleeping bears and hunting cats. Lovely as it was to have such distraction from my thoughts, the sastrugi often made life difficult. Usually I was able to ski around the largest obstacles but occasionally one group would run into the next so that it was debatable whether a detour was any better than simply ploughing through the uneven patches. Time and again I'd heave my sledges over the dips and ridges, smashing my ski tips into the fins and protrusions of solidifying snow, wading through the softness in between where drift had collected.

I revelled in the fact that the custom-made articulated sledge was working well. Not once did it roll or snag as I forced a path through the choppy ground. Nevertheless, it was hard work. I found myself panting with exertion, regularly stopping to lean on my ski poles as I sucked at the cold air through my face mask. Sometimes I'd feel as if I couldn't get enough oxygen and pulled open a wider gap in my mask to gulp mouthfuls of unfiltered and unfettered air. It was always a mistake. The air was fresh but also dry and the extremity of it caught at the back of my throat as I drank it in, making me cough violently.

I repeatedly glanced at the sky trying to judge the meteorological omens. Cloud formations shifted ominously, some of them dense and menacing, others as fine as gossamer. As they jostled restlessly in the jet streams and currents of the wind there was the permanent threat that they would once again close over me like a carapace of doom and swallow me up into that swirling insubstantial dream-world I knew so well. I watched them froth and billow at the periphery of my vision. Several times all but a gap directly overhead filled with cloud. I would resign myself to the fact that I would soon be engulfed and said longing goodbyes to the rays of warmth and light in readiness. But each time I watched in wonder as the sun seemed to melt back the edges of gloom, chasing away the threat. I sent silent bids of thanks skyward to my blazing protector.

The power of the sun was enough to keep the teeth of the wind at bay but as soon as a bank of cloud encroached on the sunlight, the wind bit through my clothing and made me shiver. Usually I wore nothing under my windproof jacket but insulated salopettes over thin thermals – the body heat created by the effort of skiing was enough to keep me warm – but lately I'd added a fleece jumper for extra insulation. It was getting noticeably colder. Despite counting down the minutes until each break and looking forward to the pleasure of a pause, I noticed that once I stopped I was increasingly eager to get moving again. If I was stationary for too long I'd get perilously cold, my body seeming to stiffen so that it felt almost impossible to drag my limbs into motion again. Even with breaks lasting no longer than a few minutes I'd set off with my ski poles trailing limply from their straps around my wrist while my hands worked my fingers inside my large padded mitts to bring them painfully back to life. Today I noticed that I was having to work my hands almost continuously even though I wore my warmest mitts. I'd repeatedly clench and re-clench my fists, curling my fingers within the warmth of my own palms, pricking each fingertip in turn with my thumbnail to make sure there was still feeling in every digit. I rarely kept my thumb in the insulated space provided for it in my mitt while I was skiing. Without the warmth of my other fingers it would get too cold very quickly. My toes too felt worrying cold for the first time. Usually they were snug all day in their felt encasing but today I had to work them constantly to keep the blood circulating.

Stopping to pitch camp I knew that kicking off my skis as usual and pressing my boots into the snow would only make my feet even colder. I moved quickly, working methodically around my tent, exaggerating my movements to keep my heart thumping and the blood moving round my body, warming my extremities. The plan worked a little too well. In a surprisingly short space of time I was wheezily out of breath, pausing to cough as the cold, dry air caught in my throat as it had done repeatedly all day. Eventually I pushed myself through the tent door, kneeling in the vestibule for a second to savour the sudden relief from the wind. I pulled the face-covering away from my skin, glad to be free, but I couldn't rest for long. Already I could feel the pinch of the cold working on my toes within my boots. I pushed sleeping mats flat on the floor of the sleeping compartment, threw my sleeping bag to the far end and placed my colour coded bags in their established places. I dug a deep trench along the length of the vestibule leaving a small shelf for my stove on its mesh board. With my feet in the trench I was able to sit upright on the edge of the sleeping compartment. Still in ice-encrusted layers and ski boots I felt the chill of cold air penetrating my clothing and shivered. Anxious for some warmth and ignoring the numb stiffness in my fingers I hastily connected a fuel bottle to the robust little stove and let out a dribble of liquid fuel in readiness to prime it. I unzipped my jacket slightly so that I could reach down through layers of fleece and thermal to where I kept my precious disposable lighter close to my chest. I pressed the lighter to the stove, feeling the sting of friction as I struck the flint with my rapidly freezing thumb.

No flame appeared.

I tilted the stove slightly to bring the flammable liquid closer to the lighter and struck again. No flame. I brought the lighter close to my face, checking there was still fuel in its see-thru chamber and giving it a good shake at the same time. Still no flame. The lighter was warm to the touch (the reason I kept it so close to my heart) and I'd been careful to keep it dry. I let out some gas before striking the flint again. Still no flame. I could see the flint spark but the gas would not ignite. Aware of my increasingly urgent need for warmth I stashed the lighter back in its place down my front and reached for my small bag of spares. I had brought three disposable lighters with me – a spare and a spare spare. I tried each in turn, warming them first – but neither would light.

I felt a rising tension of alarm. If I couldn't light my stove I would be without heat, I wouldn't be able to melt snow which would leave me without water and without water I was unable to make food. I could perhaps manage with just the chocolate and snacks I had with me but I was too far from the Pole to be able to survive without water to drink. The consequences were clear. This one small malfunction of the most humble item of kit I carried with me could mean the end of my entire expedition. All this effort, all these days of heartache and willpower and miserable perseverance could be for nothing.

Matches.

The shock of my panic had made me momentarily forget that when packing in South America I had thrown into my bags a small pot of emergency matches despite the fact that I carried no less than three disposable lighters. With my heart beating hard I struck one of the slender matchsticks. The tip broke immediately, rendering it useless. I swore. With trembling hands I struck another, barely daring to breath for fear of blowing out the tiny bobbing ball of flame. The fuel ignited and I sat watching the stove prime, unsure if it was the heat of the fire or the blush of relieved gratitude that was washing over me. I waited until the stove fizzed into full flow, the central ring glowing a fierce red, before I dared sit back and consider my problem. I hadn't expected to need the matches – they'd been thrown in as an afterthought – so I had no idea how many sticks were in the pot. Would there be enough to see me as far as the Pole and my resupply with its fresh lighters? I carefully emptied the pot of matches onto a dry section of my sleeping mat and counted them slowly, feeling the stress of anticipation as I did so. I was still 175 nautical miles from the Pole and at my current rate of progress I estimated that it would take me a minimum of thirteen days. I had to light my stove at least twice every day, so I needed at least twenty-six matches.

I think it will be indelibly engrained in my memory for the rest of my life that there were forty-six matches in the pot.

This meant I needed to ration myself to three matches per day and I would have seven to spare. In order to make my limited supply of matches last it would be critically important not to let my stove blow out in a draft, be washed out by condensation dripping from the bottom of the pot, be doused by spilt liquid or run dry of fuel before I was finished melting snow and heating water. I also couldn't afford many mis-strikes.

Having carefully replaced the matches in their water-tight container I looked again at the disposable lighters. I couldn't understand why all three should stop working at once. I had used similar lighters on all my previous expeditions and couldn't remember ever having had such a serious problem. My only thought was that it could be something to do with altitude. I didn't have an altimeter with me but my maps showed that I was climbing to the highest parts of Antarctica's domed interior and would reach altitudes of around 4,000 metres. My GPS, although an uncalibrated and unreliable measure of height, roughly agreed with the maps. Although these aren't impressive heights by mountaineering standards, the cold, dry and already thin atmosphere of Antarctica amplifies the effects of altitude. I thought back to my unusual breathlessness that day following any slight extra physical exertion and remembered that during the night I had woken with the panicky sensation of not being able to fill my lungs. For the last few nights I had found it difficult to sleep despite being physically and mentally exhausted. Perhaps I was beginning to feel the effect of altitude? If it was beginning to have an impact on my body then was it not also likely to be having an effect on my equipment?

The higher ground was also undoubtedly bringing colder temperatures. Without a thermometer I couldn't tell how low but I noticed the difference in the environment around me. Moisture hung in the air as tiny particles of ice reflecting the light which made everything sparkle as if sprinkled with glitter and the snow surface became a patchwork of flat, shiny crystals, like miniature shards of glass. My body felt the drop in temperature too. It wasn't only the sudden need to be constantly working my toes and fingers all day, but also the fact that exposure to the cold was now painful. My pee-stops had gone from being simply unpleasant to positive agony. It was impossible to remove my big mitts for more than a few seconds without the sting of numbness setting in, so I struggled with zip pulls and layers without removing them. In an effort to keep myself hydrated in the dry atmosphere I was drinking up to four litres of liquid a day which meant that I needed to pee at almost every break. Even if I faced into wind and squatted close to my sledges for shelter, the moment of exposure was never brief enough to be comfortable. I began to avoid stopping altogether, eating on the move and deliberately not drinking so much. I knew I was dehydrating myself and I knew how stupid this was (I had berated my teams often enough for similar offences). Dehydration slows the circulation and makes extremities more susceptible to the cold. Even knowing this, avoiding regular plunges into the freezing air seemed to be a more urgent matter of survival.

Before leaving the UK I had decided that for precisely this reason it was time to learn how to pee like a man. Digging out from my store of kit the small plastic device designed for the purpose, I'd stood in my bathroom at home and told myself that the key to mastering this new skill was practice. Standing on an old towel, I faced the toilet and gazed down at the loo bend as I put the funnel in place. Realising that the loo seat was in the way, I instinctively lifted it.

'Ha!' I thought in sudden understanding. 'So this is why men do that.'

It felt completely wrong to be peeing while standing up and at first I was struck with stage fright – but then I have to admit a sense of glee at this new liberation. Over the days and weeks that followed I used the device every time I needed the loo but several times I ended up peeing down my leg and throwing my jeans straight into the washing machine. There were days when I was forced to change my clothes so often that I felt like a potty training toddler. During the expedition I would have only one set of clothes that I would live in day-in, day-out, so the thought of the consequences if anything went wrong put me off using the device in earnest. I decided that, yet again, on this expedition I would stick to the old-fashioned technique and simply brave the cold.

But now that cold was so brutal that the stops brought on a kind of panic, a sense of desperation that I might be incapable of warming myself again. I was acutely aware how vulnerable I was and how narrow the margin between cold and perilously cold.

With the support of a team it is possible to push this margin to a greater extreme, working on the very limits of exhaustion, because if the worst happens there are capable team-mates to pick up the slack. On my own I was conscious that there was no one to lean on if I pushed too far, no one to put up the tent for me while I concentrated on stamping the circulation back into my feet, no one to light the stove while I kept my freezing hands in the warmth of my armpits. I had to be capable of doing all these things myself and so I was more cautious. A heightened self-awareness infiltrated every part of the expedition. I felt that I constantly needed to be thinking about what could possibly go wrong and finding ways to obviate potential calamities before they happened. I was always trying to identify my vulnerabilities so that I could do something about them, preventing myself from taking short-cuts that could prove unwise and searching for what had been forgotten or unnoticed. I crystallised this attitude into a single phrase that I repeated endlessly to myself,

'If it can go wrong, it probably will. So fix it now.'

The mantra made me pack any unused equipment safely inside my sledge bags rather than stowing it under the straps on the outside where it could potentially fall off or be blown away. It made me secure my tent to my sledge before I pitched it, no matter how slight the breeze. It made me pause every morning before skiing away from my empty campsite to glance over the snow and double check that I had left nothing behind. Even so, I still made mistakes. One evening I realised that one of my windproof overmitts, the spare I used for refuelling the stove, was missing. I still don't know how or when it escaped but it was gone. I was livid with myself for such idiotic carelessness and made fervent promises to be more meticulous.

The cold was terrifying but also spectacular. When I exhaled, my breath froze in a fine mist, settling as frost on the fur trim of my hood which I now, without fail, pulled around my face in a tightly protective oval. Frost settled on frost to form delicate feathers, extending each strand like false eyelashes. The frozen breath coated my face mask too so that when I caught glimpses of myself in the lens of my mirrored goggles it looked as if I had developed a beard of thick white stubble.

My reflection seemed strangely alien. With goggles, face mask and hood in place there was not a scrap of skin visible and I appeared more spaceman than human. The equipment became my outer skin, distancing me slightly from the environment. It was both protection and prison. While I skied, the wind flowed in a constant stream against the left side of my face, freezing the dampness from my breath so that the mask became a solid shell. It made eating a little difficult. I had to be selective about the snacks I chose from the bag in my pocket, picking out the morsels that were just the right size and shape to be posted through the breathing hole in my mask. Drinking was even worse. I'd deliberately chosen a water bottle with a protruding and narrow neck which made it easier to jam through the frozen fabric but to prevent spills I had to grip the bottle opening with my teeth to hold it in place while I gulped.

The experience of being locked inside the layers of frozen material all day reminded me of *The Man in the Iron Mask*, an old black-and-white film I had watched as a child on my grandparents' TV. The hero had been locked inside a helmet of iron in the evil hope that his own beard would eventually strangle him. The idea must have terrified me as a child because it still made me shudder as an adult and was perhaps the reason that ripping off my layers of frozen face-covering at the end of each day felt like a moment of liberation. Putting the mask back on again the next morning became a ritual of almost ceremonial importance. As I fixed each Velcro fastening and settled each seam I sank deeper into a state of readiness for the day ahead.

The mask was my polar war paint.

As I crossed into the eighty-eighth degree of latitude I met the line of longitude at 132 degrees west, the invisible line that I would follow south to the bottom of the world. This meridian is the route that all traffic in and out of the South Pole is obliged to follow, including the SPOT convoy that I judged must have passed through this same area just a few weeks before me. I started to see multiple tracks in the snow, the deep chevroned imprints sometimes bunched together in a single rutted band and at other times spread out over 200 metres or more. These loud echoes of man seemed rudely out of place in a landscape so devoid of anything human and yet I was aware that I drew comfort from this tangible proof that life was still out there somewhere. It made the Pole feel tantalisingly close.

That day, I was determined not to stop and camp until I was within one hundred nautical miles of the Pole. That was my aim but neither my cough nor my goggles were being very supportive. The cough had become a persistent irritation that hindered sleeping, and transformed skiing into a halting business of hacking and spitting. I'd be stopped in my tracks every few minutes by a coughing fit that would bend me double and leave me gasping for air with the effort, periodically spitting blood-speckled phlegm onto the snow. The heaving made my eyes water, creating uncomfortable globs of ice in my eyelashes and steaming up the lenses of my goggles. The condensation reduced my vision to a distorted haze and gradually solidified to ice. It was a sunny day and I was on the plateau, out of danger of crevasses, so I persevered with translucent vision for as long as possible before switching to my spare pair. It didn't take long for the coughing to fog up my ice-free lenses once again and I resigned myself to skiing with limited vision. So I didn't pay attention when I saw three dark areas of shade ahead of me. I assumed they were just large sastrugi. I didn't even really pay much attention when they started to swap positions with each other – by this stage I was used to seemingly stationary objects floating about. Then I felt an eerie tingle, like the shiver caused by the movement of an unexplained shadow in the darkness.

Lifting my goggles, I was momentarily blinded by the unfiltered light but as my eyes refocused on the three dark lumps I knew exactly what they were. I stopped skiing, pulled down my face mask, let my arms hang by my sides and waited for them to get closer. I knew they had seen me – I would have been visible from miles away. Sure enough as I watched they converged like heat-seeking missiles, great plumes of snow hanging in the air behind them as they bounced and plunged and ploughed through the sastrugi. In less than a minute the three oversized trucks with their half deflated wheels that I knew to be forty-four inches in diameter had stopped within metres of me. They were the very same vehicles I had driven to the Pole just the year before.

Twelve months after skiing to the South Pole with a team of women from around the Commonwealth I'd been asked to go back as support crew looking after a joint German-Austrian TV production. I was part of a three-person team that would drive modified 4x4 trucks from the coast of Antarctica to the Pole and back to transport and support two film crews. The other members of my team were Icelanders, Gisli and Gummi. The unfamiliar Icelandic names had made them sound, to me, like two of Snow White's seven dwarves. The impression was deepened when we all met for the first time; they were both bearded and ruddy. Over the following six weeks, and 6,000 kilometres, I learnt to trust my new team completely and we became good friends – friends that now appeared from the vehicles in front of me.

I had been completely alone for twenty long days but now I was greeted by wide grins and enveloped in wonderfully familiar Icelandic-sized hugs from both Gummi and Gisli. They had come to find me and I was pathetically grateful to see them. I was surprised not to be crying. The last three weeks had been so emotional that I expected such a momentous event to reduce me to a sobbing heap but some reflex kicked in, the reflex that tells us what is acceptable behaviour in public. The sudden noise and colour and movement made me feel sluggish in comparison as if my brain needed a short delay to process all the new information. Otherwise I was delighted at how easy I found it to be normal. I could see the curiosity in my friends' faces, each of them more bearded and ruddy than normal after a month in the field. They had clearly been slightly nervous about what they would find when they came looking for me.

'You look perfect – like you've been out for a day skiing!' marvelled Gisli, obviously relieved.

It wasn't the place to try and explain that it was the struggle on the inside that was the real fight. Already, wonderful as it was to see them, I was worried about what the impact of this meeting would be on my fragile emotional state.

It transpired that I was not the only reason for them to be in this part of Antarctica. They were in convoy to the coast but would be returning to the Pole in a week or so. It was deflating to think that the ground it had taken me more than three weeks to cover was no more than a few days' drive in the modified vehicles. My mind drifted longingly to the heated cabs and padded comfort of the trucks that I knew so well and my expedition suddenly seemed ridiculously punishing in contrast. Why was I putting myself through this when the same journey could be made a lot faster and with a lot less effort by other means? I remembered something the venerated desert explorer Sir Wilfred Thesiger had written: that 'to have done the journey on a camel when I could have done it in a car would have turned the venture into a stunt'.

Was that all my journey amounted to – a stunt?

When it was time to leave I felt glad that they weren't driving away from me, that instead I would be skiing away from them. This way it seemed like a positive rather than a passive action. My friends stood close by as I put on my skis and attached myself to the sledges. With a few final hugs, pats on the back and a promise that they would wait for me at the Pole I glided away, turning twice to wave. When I turned the third time it was to see that the glinting convoy was already on the move, reduced to dark lumps on the horizon before disappearing for good. Before I had skied more than a mile I was alone once again.

Perhaps it was my imagination but I like to think that Antarctica could sense that I needed some solace. The wind seemed to drop away to almost nothing and the light took on a softer tone, blushing the snow with bronze and sepia which made the landscape seem warmer and more inviting than its normal gimlet glare. The sastrugi had died away during the day so that I found myself on a blanched beach of wet silver, the surface as sleek and shiny as the coat of an animal fresh out of the water.

I thought back to the horrid days on the Leverett Glacier and the gloomy week wrapped in bad weather in the mountains, days when the Pole had seemed to be an impossible goal, when just getting out of the tent for another day had been a monumental struggle. And yet here I was with less than a hundred nautical miles to go. I couldn't imagine what would stop me now. The fear of the miles and days had melted away to be replaced by the relief of knowing that the end (of sorts) was in sight. My doubt had been hammered and hectored into belief. Finally.

As I skied I spent hours visualising the moment of arrival at the South Pole, how it would feel to lay my hands on that silver sphere once again knowing that this time I had brought myself there alone and under my own steam. The thought spurred me on but never once did my imagination venture beyond the Pole, to the distances and experiences that waited for me on the other side of Antarctica. Unconsciously, my mind was protecting itself.

Away to my left a solar column fell from the sun to the horizon like a laser, the point of apparent contact marked by a semi-circular glow. It was an optical effect I had seen before on the epic flatness of the polar plateau but this time it felt symbolic, as if it was a glimpse of a personal protector that trailed my movements as closely and as effortlessly as a shadow. It glided along the horizon, spatially in the far distance and yet intimately near, travelling beside me in silent companionship.

I have always loved the idea that no two people see the same rainbow. The optical effect I see from the position of my eyes is dictated by the laws of physics to be unique, different from the view of anyone else, even if they are standing right beside me. My rainbow is unique to me, a fact that transforms it into a magical personal secret.

Even if I hadn't been alone, the sprite that accompanied me on the horizon was mine and mine only – a guardian angel that would see me safe to the Pole and perhaps even to the far side of Antarctica.

CHAPTER FIVE

LIFE RAFT

@felicity_aston Roald Amundsen reached the South Pole 100 years ago today. Sadly, I'm still a degree and a half away.

@felicity_aston Brushing the ice out of the fur ruff that trims the hood of my jacket. It's like grooming a dog.

@felicity_aston Cold day. I was frozen into my jacket all day because my breath had turned to ice all over the zip at my chin!

I can't remember the first time I heard about Scott of the Antarctic. It seems like he has always been there, lodged in my childhood consciousness alongside the folklore heroes of Robin Hood and King Arthur. The story of Scott's long trek to the South Pole to find that the Norwegians had beaten him to it, followed by the tragic death of his party just miles from safety on the desperate return journey, contains so many memorable scenes of fortitude and stoicism that it has almost taken on the cadence of a parable. But I have come to realise that it is a history that has been streamlined with the telling through the generations. The individual episodes of adventure that make up the story are like pebbles on a beach that start life as boulders of irregular and complex form but over time are smoothed and simplified until they become oval stones that fit perfectly in the hand. Their new shape is pleasing and easy to handle, yet they have lost something in the process.

Like countless others, as a child I tried to imagine the hardship experienced by Scott and his men and marvelled at the heroic endurance recorded in journals and accounts but ultimately, true empathy was impossible. Scott and his expedition were men of a foreign age with attitudes that were largely unrecognisable to me at the opposite end of the twentieth century. I admired their actions but felt distinctly removed from them as people. It's impossible to say what impact the story of Scott may have had on my choices and decisions in life, any more than it is possible to isolate the precise legacy of Enid Blyton's *Famous Five* books that I devoured greedily as a child or the influence of watching intrepid BBC TV presenters pluckily tackling adventurous stunts on *Blue Peter*. I can't claim to feel a direct debt of inspiration to Scott.

I hope that, were he able to witness some of the polar journeys taking place today, Scott might recognise the same spirit of adventure alive and well but I doubt he, nor any man of his day, would have been able to conceive that a woman would have any interest whatsoever in travelling to Antarctica herself, much less ski across it. They are heroes to me, but not role models.

What I can credit the stories of Scott for is my first introduction to a place that has inspired me for as long as I can remember. I found the thought of such a cold, empty continent instantly and irresistibly thrilling. At school as a teenager when working towards my first raft of qualifications, I was given the option to provide a topic for a significant part of my geography coursework and Antarctica was my immediate choice. Later, curiosity about such an extreme environment led me to seek out my first polar adventure, a youth expedition to Greenland. Later still, when looking for a job as a graduate, I sought out any career opportunity that would allow me to see this almost unimaginable land at the bottom of the world for myself. Looking back on my life so far, Antarctica, and the desire to know it, seems to be a constant thread running through everything, giving shape to the whole. To date, it's hard to think of any place, person or object which has captured my enthusiasm and energies so thoroughly and instinctively.

I grew up in the south east of England, where winters were normally grey, drizzling affairs; but occasionally it would snow, transforming the familiar woods and fields around my childhood home into an unfamiliar middle-earth of blanketed topography and muted sounds. Dressed in Wellington boots and brightly coloured gloves, my sister and I would go exploring in this new world, discovering marshy ponds turned into skating-rinks, dripping water transformed into stalactites of ice, snow-laden trees forming tunnels into secret places and the invisible life of the countryside exposed as tracks in the newly laid carpet of white. Snow meant days off school, snowball fights, sledging and warming fingers that thrummed with cold on mugs of sweet hot drinks in front of the fire at home. Our house was a little way out of the nearest town, set back from the main road without any immediate neighbours. A heavy fall of snow would sometimes temporarily cut us off, something

I found agonisingly exciting. Once it even caused a power cut and for months afterwards at every given opportunity I would breathlessly relate how we had been forced to cook on camping stoves in the kitchen by torchlight. Against the backdrop of my limited childhood experiences, this was the pinnacle of dramatic adventure.

This connection between snow and an expectation of delicious excitement, coupled with stories of gallant polar explorers, developed over time into an understanding that Antarctica meant adventure. I came to believe that Antarctica was somewhere you went to test yourself, not only against nature but against your true character. I expected that the demands of an Antarctic experience would leave nowhere to hide, that it would expose the inner qualities of a person – both their strengths and their weaknesses. Part of me felt nervous that I might prove myself inept, but the risk of unearthing uneasy truths about myself seemed small in comparison to the excitement at the challenge and the opportunity to discover what my personal qualities might be. I came to view Antarctica as a testing ground that would allow me to understand my potential and my vulnerabilities, an understanding that might, over time, enable me to become a better version of myself.

I'm the sort of person that, when reading about the exploits of others, is distracted by curiosity to know if I would be able to do the same. How would I have reacted in that situation? Would I be the hero leading the way and helping others, or the one paralysed by helpless panic, or the one driven by terror to make selfish decisions? It is this curiosity that motivates me to explore where my personal capabilities and limits lie, and which draws me to ever more challenging expeditions. I want to know who I am. Not that I am driven to prove myself a hero. It is in fact the exact opposite. I am driven by the fear that I will find myself lacking, and this fear pushes me to search for reassurance.

It strikes me that we all tend to be fascinated by our own nature, that we are always looking for a way to learn more about who we are. Methods are as diverse as ancient rites of passage and horoscopes, art and alternative therapies but the appeal is the same; we are drawn to the promise of discovering something new about ourselves. It was this desire for self-understanding that had led me to adventures in Antarctica as a graduate, but it was the suspicion of what such self-understanding might reveal that had lured me back to Antarctica alone. Through the prism of that alone-ness I hoped to establish once and for all if my fears were founded, the fear that – at my core – I was not up to it.

I must have pondered all this every single day as I skied. I had hours to explore every avenue of thought on the matter but I was now so close to the Pole that it seemed as if I caught the occasional faint rumble of machinery drifting towards me on the wind. This unlikely echo of civilisation seemed plausible because the South Pole is currently the site of one of the largest scientific research stations on the continent. The Amundsen–Scott station at the South Pole was established in 1957 by the American Navy and has been slowly expanding ever since. There are now around 250 people that live and work there in a giant, three-storey, E-shaped building on stilts during the summer season, a population that shrinks to 100 for the long, dark winter. In summer the station is busy with minibuses and transport snowmobiles (weird-looking contraptions that haul groups of people standing in a double row while clinging to a specially built sledge) moving people from the main station building to the outlying science facilities like extreme subzero commuters. Huge cargo planes arrive frequently, landing spectacularly on a broad skiway running along one side of the station, their sucking engines beating the air while they are unloaded. The engines are never stopped for fear that they will never start again in the severe cold.

This was to be my third arrival at the South Pole though each occasion had been very different. The last time I had arrived at ninety degrees south I had driven into the Pole with my Icelandic friends and a convoy of vehicles but my first, and inevitably most precious, sight of the South Pole had been when skiing in with the team of women I had created and trained myself. The station had been distinctly visible as a dark, hard-edged dash on the horizon from a distance of just over twelve nautical miles. Now, as I drew near to this magic number once again, my eyes darted restlessly between every hint of light and shade in the distance. Every time I saw a suspect dash I'd glare at it fixated, remaining sceptical that it was the Pole and yet simultaneously hopeful.

Towards the end of my twenty-fifth day of skiing, the dash I had been glaring at since my last break refused to disappear. I deliberately looked away several times, each time challenging myself to find the same dark shape on the horizon. I moved my goggles to make sure it wasn't simply a scratch on my lens. After an hour it disappeared. I'd had too many false alarms to feel either surprised or disappointed. Instead I registered my sledge growing heavier – a sign that I was climbing an undetectable incline. After a while, the sledge grew lighter and, once more, I spotted the same dark grey dash. It hadn't disappeared at all, it had just been temporarily obscured from view as I climbed uphill. I stopped in my ski tracks and stood silently as the realisation floated softly downwards through my brain, settling like sediment. I was looking at the South Pole. My grin made the flesh of my cheeks press dangerously against the ice of my frozen face mask. I wanted to laugh and to cry but instead I did neither. I merely stood and stared and let the sediment fall.

The next morning I could barely wait to leap out of the tent and check if the dark dash was still there. I stood facing the sharp, steady wind from the Pole and focused on the horizon, sensing a fizz of panic that I had simply willed the dash into being. Then I saw it. With the sun now in the opposite half of the sky it appeared closer and clearer than it had the day before. I knew from my GPS that I was a good day's ski away but the dash appeared to be tantalisingly close, leading me to believe that I could suspend the laws of physics and cover the remaining miles in no more than an hour or two. As I dismantled the tent and packed my sledges I was aware of anticipation escalating inside me like a winding dynamo. I mentally cautioned myself to stick to the regular routine, to stay steady, but it was futile. In my mind I was already at the Pole and my body was rushing to catch up, impatient to chase the horizon. I skied cheerfully, my face taking on a fixed rictus of glee, my eyes unable to move from the dash. The more I looked at it, the more detail I recognised. It was undoubtedly the station building, long and rectangular, as I remembered it. I searched the horizon either side hoping to see the two big white domes housing satellite dishes which had been such an unmissable landmark the last time I approached the station by ski. I couldn't see them but reasoned that this must be because I was approaching from the opposite direction.

I could feel that I was pushing forward faster and harder than usual but every detail of the landscape around me seemed abnormally distinct. Tiny bobbles of frost covered the surface of the snow that flashed by under my skis. It looked as if Antarctica had shivered and been left with goosebumps. Glancing behind me I noticed for the first time a bank of cloud puffed thickly in the middle-distance. I was being stalked by bad weather and it made me push on even harder towards the dash which was now a thick oblong so close that I could make out structural details and even windows. I couldn't see any of the containers or outlying buildings that I remembered but put this down to perspective or perhaps a change at the station since my last visit.

Feeling curiously nervous about my imminent arrival I went through a mental check list of the strict rules issued by the station and passed on to me by Steve at Union Glacier about skiing into and out of the South Pole. In past decades the station management had become exasperated with expeditions and explorers arriving at the Pole without the means to look after themselves, often needing medical assistance and occasionally lacking any way to get home. Understandably, the station pointed out that it was not an unofficial Search and Rescue service for polar adventurers but a government-funded scientific research facility. As a result the station now goes to great lengths to separate the two functions of the South Pole. If I arrived at the base as an employee of the British Antarctic Survey or any other governmental organisation undertaking science in Antarctica, in the spirit of international co-operation that is fundamental on the continent, I would reasonably expect to be welcomed into the station buildings, provided with accommodation, food and any other logistical support I might need. Arriving as a private individual, the situation was very different. Visitors are welcome to the Pole but only within strict boundaries. It doesn't matter if you have flown into the South Pole on a private jet for a photoshoot or skied alone across the continent, there is no access to the station or to the people that work there beyond an organised tour of the station building that can be arranged on request. Medical staff at the station would not hesitate to provide assistance to anyone in need in an emergency but expeditions are told not to expect or to ask for any kind of support including use of facilities or any top-up of supplies. Quite rightly, expeditions are obliged to look after themselves.

An area a short distance away from the South Pole and the main station building had been set aside for visitors arriving who wished to camp while they waited for flights back to the coast to basecamps like Union Glacier. This was where I expected to find the resupply bag I had prepared for myself and where I knew it was likely I would see other expedition teams that had either just finished their journey or were waiting to start.

The rules surrounding my arrival and departure from the South Pole dictated my route (I was asked to follow the line of longitude 132 degrees west) but also my ablutions. Forming a circle 200 kilometres across, the last degree of latitude around the Pole is a strict no-poo zone. All human waste has to be deposited in special bags and carried away. I had been making deposits into ziplock bags for the past week and had them safely stowed, frozen, in the bottom of my sledges under the sledge bags. Within the boundary of the South Pole station it is also a no-pee zone. I'd been told to carry a pee-bottle with me as I approached and to deposit the contents later at an appropriate facility within the station compound. However, as the oblong got closer it occurred to me that I didn't want to have to pull down my trousers to pee within sight of staff at the base, bottle or no. I waited until I was as close as I dared before stopping for what I hoped would be my last loo break.

Moving off again, the station was so close that I could see sunlight reflecting from its windows and a flash of light that I decided must be a camera flash. I noticed the cloud that had been behind me slowly creep over the sun, making me shiver and almost instantly flattening the contrast. The air between me and the South Pole grew hazy, so that the edges of everything appeared watery and washed out, like abstract watercolours. The station was strangely quiet. I hadn't seen a single vehicle.

I stopped dead in horror.

I was close enough to see that this wasn't the Amundsen–Scott station at all.

Tears of frustration rose instantly and I felt a sense of desperation more vengeful than during my very first few hours alone. It was like I was right back on the Leverett Glacier. As the cloud thickened around me, reducing the visibility with the sure determination of a dimming switch, I saw that my dark oblong was not the South Pole, it wasn't even a building. It was two of the immense fuel bladders dragged by the SPOT traverse. Their rubbery skin ribbed with reinforced seams had glinted in the sun like metal and in the empty landscape they had looked much bigger, than they were in reality. They had been abandoned in the snow by the convoy, still bloated with fuel, presumably for storage until they were needed. Like a tourist pictured holding up Big Ben or squishing the Eiffel Tower with their thumb, it was a trick of scale and perspective. A bad navigator forces their surroundings to fit a map in order to prove they are going in the right direction. I had ignored

Completely covered to protect my skin from freezing in extreme sub-zero temperatures, I looked more alien than human.

Seeing the scale of the crevasse fields as we flew over the Transantarctic Mountains was frightening.

Camped on the Leverett Glacier beneath Mount Beazley – before it got windy. The route up to the Antarctic Plateau is just visible to the far left.

Marking the position of my camp on the map – for morale more than navigation.

Tweeting via SMS on the Iridium phone. It was a one-way form of communication but became important psychologically.

Reaching the geographic South Pole for the third time in my life – this time having skied more than 600 kilometres alone.

My tent dwarfed by the vastness of the plateau, a place completely
without life of any form.

The sun was in the sky 24 hours a day, circling endlessly overhead.

Thiel Mountains, the first geography I'd seen in more than
800 kilometres.

A perfect Antarctic day with clear skies and no wind, making it warm enough to be able to sit outside and enjoy the view in a rare moment of calm.

Skiing across Antarctica was far more of a mental and emotional challenge than a physical one.

The sun above Wilson's Nunatak looking magnificent with a circular rainbow around it, an optical effect known as a halo.

Antarctica is riddled with fissures that can be hundreds of metres deep. This one is clearly visible but the majority are hidden by snow and impossible to see in bad weather.

The plane sent to take me home – a sight I had been simultaneously longing for and dreading.

Finished.

all the warning signs and turned my desire into reality even though what I saw didn't fit what I knew. The lack of the satellite domes, the lack of outlying buildings, the lack of movement. Antarctica had fooled me. As if to match my mood, the weather closed in, stealthy and silent, until I was enclosed in a private, melancholic world of grey.

My brain wearily digested this latest blow as the wind rose from nothing into a gale in what felt like a few minutes. I paused to force the zip of my jacket right up to the top of my collar so that the fur of my hood tightly enclosed my face and offered some protection. Through my goggles I could see a fur rimmed oval, a confined porthole looking out onto a nacreous mass of shifting light and snow-choked air. I pulled out my GPS and saw that there were still several nautical miles between me and the Pole. Trudging forward I relapsed into a glum routine, skiing for ninety minutes before stopping for a reluctant break, shaking the blood furiously into my hands as I continued on. It was warmer now than it had been a week ago on the highest parts of the plateau but the wind seemed to drive in the cold, like the wet chill of a dark winter's night at home by the English coast that enters the bones no matter how many layers are worn. I stared forward as I skied although there was nothing to focus on and became aware of that familiar, dizzy vertigo making my head spin. I searched for any slight contrast in the snow beneath my skis as I passed over it or for some hint of a horizon, no matter how faint, to try and stabilise the spinning sensation. Instead I caught the suggestion of a shadow in the flurries. It had sharp edges like my old friends LOO-JW and SPT-11 but was bigger. As I got closer I could see that it was a large, yellow, rectangular sign with writing on it. It stood completely alone, isolated in space by the blizzard as if dropped randomly from the sky. I skied towards it until I could make out the words in black paint,

'Welcome to the South Pole'

I stood confused for a moment. I knew from my GPS that I was still some way off from the Pole. I peered around the sign, squinting into the increasingly dense whiteout for any sign of the station but could see nothing. If the station was ahead it was completely obscured by the snow being flung around in the wind. The farce of my situation emerged through my confusion. The scene had all the absurdity of a Monty Python sketch. If it wasn't for the blizzard it might have even been funny.

I was eager to be moving again. As I skied away from the yellow sign I could feel excitement building and noticed that I was skiing faster than was wise but I repressed my misgivings. Within striking distance of the end, my pace and my reserves of energy didn't matter, I told myself. My only thought was to get there as quickly as possible. The grey haze had grown so thick that it started to look dirty brown. I still couldn't see any sign of the station but flags appeared out of the gloom on my right like a line of ghostly shadows standing to attention. I could barely see one flag from the next but it raised my hopes that at any minute I'd see something I recognised.

I knew from previous arrivals that navigating the Amundsen–Scott base is a complicated affair. Having skied in more or less a straight line for hundreds of kilometres, within the station's perimeters I was obliged to follow specific routes marked by flags to avoid wandering into science projects, active runways or forbidden parts of the base. My heart sank as I spotted a junction of not one but three flag lines up ahead, each identical and each heading in a completely different direction. Without being able to see the station building I had no idea which one to follow. I looked for any clues on the ground. Skiing over to the flagline on my right I thought I could feel a groomed surface under my skis, the snow was hard packed like a track. The direction also fitted what I remembered of the station map. Happy with my decision I set off along the flagline, eager not to waste any more time – but within a few hundred metres I stopped. I remembered how easily I'd been fooled by the fuel bladders earlier that day. The thought of another stupid mistake causing me to ski pointless kilometres in the wrong direction made me pause. A vision formed of skiing right out of the Pole altogether and finding myself out on the polar plateau having missed the station in the bad weather. The premonition caused a shudder. Not only did I need to make the station to collect my resupply of food and fuel, I was mentally clinging to the promise of company, of respite from the claustrophobia of my alone-ness. I reluctantly unzipped my jacket to search for my GPS, letting in a rush of cold air and the unpleasant wetness of driving snow that made me wince in discomfort. Shuffling forward on my skis to get a reading, the small unit flashed a thick black arrow on screen pointing straight towards me like an accusation of stupidity. The South Pole was in exactly the opposite direction. I had followed the wrong flagline.

I tried to repress the surge of frustrated annoyance and remain calm as I skied back to the junction. I inspected the remaining two flaglines, neither of which headed in the direction indicated by my GPS to the Pole. I stood listening to the howl of the wind through the flag canes, watching the snow being whipped past my face and felt enraged into a fury of self-pity. Why did this have to be so complicated?

Feeling shamefully sorry for myself, I stomped towards the flagline on my left. I would follow this line of flags to their bitter end, I thought truculently, regardless of where they went. They must, after all, lead somewhere. I set off recklessly fast without pausing to replace my face-covering properly. I was blind to caution in my haste to push forward. I felt the same sense of panicky anticipation that comes when late for an important interview. I skied on and on, aware that the ventilation zips of my jacket were open and letting in snow, aware that my goggles were so iced up that I could barely see, feeling my jacket uncomfortably riding up under my sledge harness, noticing that my sledge bag was a little open letting spindrift blow inside it. I did nothing about any of these potential disasters, blinded by my hurry to be at the Pole and made stupid by my desperation. The snow under my skis felt soft and deep where drifts had formed banks and mounds. It didn't seem that there had been much traffic along the flagline, which worried me, but I wouldn't allow myself to dwell on the thought – as if I could ensure I was going in the right direction by stubbornness alone.

After what seemed to be hours of effort I still wasn't sure I was travelling in the right direction and there was still nothing to be seen in the haze ahead. I was hungry and thirsty having not stopped for a break, I was uncomfortable from my clothing being neglected and I was exhausted, both physically and mentally. I had had enough. I threw down my ski poles and roared at the wind. It wasn't fair to face such frustration when I was so close to the end. Feeling utterly sorry for myself I burst into tears, ripping off my goggles and face mask to yell at the weather in anger. I wanted nothing but to be able to stop. I wanted to sit on the ground and let the snow cover me. I didn't care about the cold, about frostbite or dehydration or hypothermia. I would accept anything as long as it meant that all this effort and discomfort and frustration would stop.

The yelling and the tears exorcised some of the anger. After the tantrum I felt deflated and just a little embarrassed. Antarctica was not going to stop; the weather would not pause for me. The South is relentless and that is both its challenge and its lethal edge. It was up to me to see myself through this last trial. There was no reason why the last hour would not be as difficult as any other and the conditions were as dangerous within the station compound as they had been at any other point of my journey. My proximity to safety didn't make me safe. I realised I had been lured into a false sense of the end, that I'd relaxed my self-discipline in anticipation of an arrival that was realistically still a good ski away. I needed to press a mental reset button, sort myself out and start again.

Still snivelling I took off my harness and started from my base layer outwards, zipping up collars, tucking in edges, and patting Velcro securely in place. I refastened the ventilation zips on my jacket and scooped the snow out of my sledge bag. I had something to eat and something to drink before replacing my face mask and putting on a new pair of goggles to give me ice-free vision. Then I set off, noting the time so that I could stop after ninety minutes as usual. I felt relieved from the panicky anticipation that had made me taut and anxious beforehand, as if I'd been released from the coils of a large snake that had been gently but insidiously squeezing the sense out of me.

In my head I reassured myself in a series of commands: 'One way or another you will arrive at the Pole today. You will not get lost. If you miss the Pole in this weather, you will see it tomorrow when things are clearer. You will be perfectly comfortable spending another night alone. You have food, you have fuel. You will be safe.'

I imagined the worst possible scenario that might arise and then methodically lectured myself on all the reasons, firstly, why this scenario was unlikely and, secondly, why I would easily be able to get myself back on track. I became so absorbed in my thoughts that when a dense silhouette loomed out of the blowing snow it made me jump. I could make out a curved edge and recognised it as one of the domed satellite dish buildings that surround the station. Within a hundred metres the dome had sunk back into the blizzard but it didn't matter. I drew solace from the sight even though it didn't mean I wasn't skiing right past the station and back out onto the plateau. I returned to my thoughts and to my comforting internal monologue. Keeping the flagline close to my right-hand side, I fixed my gaze on my ski tips, refusing to look up even as I thought I sensed a miniscule improvement in the light.

Finally, after what felt like endless hours, a huge dark mass rose out of the gloom and I recognised the blunt end of the Amundsen–Scott station. My brain made rapid calculations. I decided I must be directly opposite the main entrance of the station on the far side of the runway. I looked for the beacon telling me where I could cross the skiway and guided my eyes forward to where I knew the ceremonial silver ball surrounded by flags should be that marks the South Pole.

I slowed my pace as I skied those last few hundred metres, enjoying the sense of relief that pulsed through me in waves. It was as if each part of me took its individual turn to relax. My body and my mind had been on high-alert for twenty-six days and for 625 kilometres but now, at last, I was safe. Safe from the cold and safe from the alone-ness. It was like grabbing hold of a life raft after being adrift at sea. The frustrations of the past few hours were forgotten and replaced with a deep sense of satisfaction: I had made it.

I was greeted by a cluster of waving figures a short distance from the Pole near the visitors' camp. It was my friends from the Icelandic convoy, returned from the coast, and they had been waiting for me as promised. The wind propelled snow between us so that it was impossible to talk to each other but I could hear muffled cheers of congratulations as I was enfolded in hugs and slapped appreciatively on the back. After a few minutes I was allowed to ski forward alone, still pulling my sledges, so that I could cover the last few feet and lay my hands on the silver sphere. For most people, this moment is the conclusion of the journey, an experience of ultimate triumph. The last time I had approached this sphere on skis I had been filled with pride and gratification. I expected to feel the same again but noticed something slightly different. This time, reaching the Pole was a pitstop, a marker in the course of a larger journey not yet half-completed.

I don't think it would ever be possible to arrive at the South Pole after a long journey to get there and not feel a sense of occasion, but as I saw my reflection in the sphere's curved surfaces I was aware of a reaction approaching resentment. It suddenly seemed ridiculous that this gaudy bauble of a monument should be the cause of so much heartache and trial. In that moment it struck me that the Pole had taken on the role of nefarious siren, luring me and dozens of others, year after year, to give so much of themselves for the reward of laying their hands on this makeshift marker at the end of the Earth. It was teacher but also tormentor. With the promise of profound revelations and new wisdom it had enticed those pioneering explorers a century ago just as it seduced new generations now.

I stood alone at the Pole staring down in baffled annoyance at my own distorted reflection, surrounded by the fury of an Antarctic blizzard. The livid colours of the flags that snapped on their poles arranged in a semi-circle around the space were dulled by the oppression of snow and cloud. Despite the noisy rage of the wind I was given a moment of odd clarity. I too, like so many others, had fallen for the addictive attraction of the Pole and I wondered anew what exactly this specific point in space represented for me that was so important I would put myself through such emotional turmoil to reach it. It suddenly seemed that the Pole itself was responsible for bringing me here and for all the trials of the past weeks.

I noticed my unexpected feelings with interest and sensed a deeper question forming but this was not the time to ponder it. As if defying a tyrant I turned my back on the silver sphere to face my friends who were waiting close by. They handed me the British flag from the selection surrounding the Pole and I stood in triumphant pose as they took the expected pictures. The flag was heavy with the resistance of the wind in its billowing material and as I fought against the incompliant weather a stranger in a red padded parka emerged from the blowing snow. His hood was pulled down low over his face and the wind buffeted him so forcefully that he stumbled towards us like a drunk from the direction of the station. It was unusual for anyone from the station to greet a non-official arrival at the Pole, so it was with great surprise that, as the stranger patted me on the back, I felt an illicit apricot being pressed into my palm.

Another member of staff made a rather more dramatic arrival in one of the station's monumental tractors. Jumping from the cab she handed me a bag containing a clutch of fresh basil, a nectarine and (more practically) a pack of baby wipes with which I was instructed to indulge myself with 'a proper wash'. I was amazed that these kindly strangers would not only take the time to come and greet me but would do so in the worst of weather. I was touched and grateful.

Eventually I let myself be led away from the Pole by my friends towards the visitors' camp nearby. Although my original plan had been not to spend any time at the Pole, during the long, lonely days on the plateau I had lured myself onwards with the promise of a rest day when I arrived. Now, there was no question of leaving immediately. I revelled in the sensation of release that came alongside the security that is concomitant with being around other people. Warmth, food, shelter, company and safety were readily available without effort or thought on my part. I spent an entire day indulging in freedom from the pressure of having to look after myself, freedom from the exhausting responsibility of having to be aware of every action and its potential consequences. The respite felt like a drug and I drifted through my chores like a contented sleepwalker. I emptied my sledges, purging them of rubbish and poo bags and my one remaining ration bag before carefully refilling them with supplies for the next leg of my journey. In the resupply bags I had prepared for myself I found not only rations and stove fuel but a fresh set of underwear, new lighters (all of which worked when I anxiously tested them) and a small bag of foody treats (a small round of soft cheese and some salty corn snacks) that I devoured on the spot.

Riffling through supplies and equipment left at the Pole by previous expeditions already finished and gone home I was delighted to find not one, but two large boxes of matches. It would be enough to last me for the entire journey if the lighters refused to ever produce fire again. Curiously my three original malfunctioning lighters had begun to splutter back to life as I had slowly descended towards the pole from the highest parts of the plateau but they still weren't reliable enough to depend on.

Several people inspected my dodgy ski binding. The consensus was that to try and detach the binding might leave me with a damaged ski and it was unlikely any reattachment in the field would be any better than the current alignment. The realisation that I would have to continue with the skis as they were was disheartening. Over the past few weeks I had cheered myself with the thought that the problem would be solved at the Pole. Now I faced the prospect of another 1,100 kilometres with the constant threat of a revolt from my knees against the toe-out duck-walk that I had evolved into using.

My dodgy ski wasn't the only reason why the thought of continuing towards the coast left me with a heavy sense of dread. Ever since my arrival at the Pole I'd been aware of the shadow of my departure. After the experience of the previous weeks I was viscerally conscious of precisely what skiing alone in Antarctica entailed. I knew what it felt like to be a solitary speck in that immense emptiness and I knew the despair of that peculiar kind of absolute alone-ness. Skiing out of the Pole would be very different from being left by the plane. I now realised that at the start of the expedition I'd had little true understanding of what I'd be facing. Once the plane had disappeared I'd had no realistic option but to keep going. Having reached the Pole, arranging to fly back to Union Glacier on one of the relatively regular flights to and from the coast wouldn't be difficult. Neither was there any shame in returning home having ended my expedition at the Pole. I had skied a respectable distance alone and could be satisfied with that. There would be no disgrace in explaining that I had gone to Antarctica to find my limits and that this was where I had found them. In contrast, if I skied out of the Pole I would be alone entirely by my own choice and with a full understanding of what waited for me. Having grasped this miraculous life raft gleefully, I was facing the realisation that I would have to release it again in order to swim for shore.

The realisation made me wary of relaxing too much; I couldn't afford to let my guard down completely. As much as I appreciated the feel and security of company in the visitors' camp I avoided socialising in the mess tent – I wasn't ready to talk about my experiences yet, as if I might hex myself for the journey still to come. Instead I sat with my friends from the convoy and listened to them sharing their stories with each other, happy to blend into the background surrounded by noise and laughter. I produced my precious clutch of basil in thanks for their hospitality which was added to the dehydrated meal for taste and divided the apricot into small sections to be passed around like hors d'oeuvres. The fragment of fruit I popped into my mouth might have been tiny but it was as flavoursome and juicy as a ripe berry.

During the long emotional ski from the Leverett Glacier I'd all but made the decision that I would not continue beyond the Pole. Just as the tides beat out a global rhythm that cannot be resisted, however, I found that the momentum of my journey wouldn't be stopped. I drifted through my rest day unwilling or unable to give the decision the thought it deserved. It seemed unreal that I was to return to that state of high-alert that I had so recently thrown off. Already my memory of the anguish I had felt every morning was softening. Could it really have felt so bad?

As if to prove that I must surely be mistaken, Antarctica looked benignly beautiful on the morning of my departure. The sky was such a dense, solid blue that I could have believed it was a painted ceiling. The light that poured from the sky and bounced from the snow was so intense that everything appeared unnaturally defined, as if every atom was visible. The station buildings stood out against the snow like paper cut-outs.

As I readied my skis and sledges to leave, a little crowd from the visitors' camp gathered to wave me off. I was presented with a leaving gift, a lightweight plastic jar of peanut butter. With weight so critical there were few presents I would have been prepared to carry, but for peanut butter I was willing to make an exception. I tucked it preciously into the safety of my sledge bags. With goodbyes completed I pushed the toe of each boot into its clamp on their respective skis, snapped shut the clasp of my harness and pushed my fists, in turn, through the wrist-loops of my ski poles. Each familiar motion of preparation was like a hammer-blow to a delicate carapace of security that had formed during my thirty-six hours at the Pole, leaving me once again exposed to the reality of Antarctica. The voices of apprehension that had plagued me every morning since leaving the Ross Ice Shelf were once again screaming through my brain. With effort I could quieten them but I couldn't switch them off completely. Leaving felt so very wrong. I had expected that having friends at the Pole would make it harder to tear myself away but in fact, if they hadn't been stood there expectantly I might never have mustered the gumption to leave at all. It is very difficult to tell a waiting crowd that you have changed your mind.

I skied forward, turning to wave at first then forcing myself to face the view ahead and not glance back. My eyes sought out the horizon, coming to rest on a slick of silver reflection beneath the sun. Without deflecting my gaze I reached up to seal the last layer of my face-covering, pressing home the Velcro so that, once more, I was isolated within my frozen mask, my private protective shell. Inside I felt hollow but contentedly so. Feeling empty seemed manageable and it was a relief to notice that thought was almost entirely absent. I concentrated instead on pushing one ski in front of the other, getting used to the new weight in my sledges, feeling the familiar stretch in my muscles and burn of cold in my lungs. The snow looked smooth under the varnish-like gloss of the sun but the appearance was deceptive. It tugged gently but insistently at my sledges every time I pushed forward as if the runners underneath stuck repeatedly to the surface.

At my first break I turned to find that the South Pole had shrunk to a cluster of Lego-bricks in the distance and by my second break it had disappeared completely. I was surprised how quickly it had vanished from view. Since leaving the Transantarctic Mountains I had been surrounded by a landscape devoid of scale or significant feature which left me blind to my progress hour to hour, day to day. It was encouraging to see, physically, what three hours of skiing meant in terms of distance travelled. As I sent wistful psychic goodbyes to the station just beyond the horizon I celebrated the fact that I was no longer on the 'wrong side' of Antarctica. This side of the Pole was closer to the main logistical hubs at the coast and more regularly crossed by planes and convoys. Travelling north rather than south brought with it a certain sense of psychological connection to the outside world, but at the same time there was an obvious absence in the scenery before me. The ground ahead was completely unmarked by any human presence. Gone were the tracks left by the SPOT vehicles which had been increasingly visible as I got closer to the Pole. No longer was I confined to following the 132 degrees west line of longitude to oblige station rules and I was struck by an invigorating sense of freedom. This part of my journey had greater footfall but ironically it was here that I felt most uninhibited because I was free to choose any direction I pleased. This was the feeling I had imagined when gazing down at the crinkled surface of Antarctica from the plane all those weeks ago. Sudden but lasting exhilaration seemed to flow into my muscles, making them feel strengthened and inexhaustible. It was impossible to imagine, in that moment, that my body would ever cease to move forward. I felt like I could keep going for ever.

I don't know when exactly I noticed that my shadow was missing. Usually it hovered ahead of me through the day, moving from my right elbow to my left as the hours progressed but now that I skied north it was gone. When the thought that had been growing reached the front of my brain, I spun round in curiosity. Sure enough my shadow now lagged behind. I turned back to the sun and considered it suspiciously. My mind balked at trying to fathom the spherical trigonometry involved but there was no denying that the sun had changed its apparent position in the sky. Whereas before it had hovered always at the periphery of my vision on one side or the other, it now blazed up ahead like the brightest of street lights on the darkest of nights. I smiled. Swapping my shadow for the sun couldn't be anything but a fair deal. I liked the idea of skiing towards this eternal symbol of brightness and optimism. The sun on my face made Antarctica seem charmingly friendly that day, aided by the fact that the wind was no more than the lightest of breezes. It left a stillness so quiet that the sussurance of my skis cutting through the light surface snow sounded as intrusive as a powerdrill. I could hear the sharp squeak of my ski poles piercing the snow pack in turn and the rush of my breath was clear enough to make out the slight rattle of spit and the resonance of my heartbeat.

Out of this imperfect silence rose a burble of numbers. They gathered in my brain like swarming insects and intruded on my contented emptiness. The number of days, the number of kilometres, the number of miles, the number of degrees, the number of kilometres divided into the number of days, the number of weeks divided into the number of degrees, the number of ration bags, the number of hours until I stopped for the day, the number of minutes until my next break, the number of strides in each minute – and then back to the number of days. It was an endlessly absorbing cycle and I stretched my arithmetical ability to its limit with the complexity of my calculations. No matter how I manipulated the numbers, what was clear was that I didn't have enough time to reach the far coast before the end of the Antarctic season.

I knew that on 26 January the camp at Union Glacier would close and everyone on the ice would leave before the planes ran any risk of getting caught in the onset of winter. The date was my absolute deadline. Wherever I was in the days leading up to 26 January, regardless of whether or not I had completed my traverse of the continent, a plane would be sent to fetch me and I would be leaving Antarctica.

It was now 22 December and my original plan had been to be far beyond the Pole by this stage but as well as the weather delay to my start, the first leg of the expedition had taken me six days longer than expected. I was seriously behind schedule. So far, I had skied 625 kilometres but I still had at least 1,100 kilometres to cover. It had taken me twenty-six days to reach the Pole and I now had only thirty-eight days left to attempt almost twice the distance. It was impossible.

That evening, during my regular call to Union Glacier to report my position, I asked to speak to Steve. He knew my question before I'd had a chance to ask it.

'Don't even think about giving up because of time,' he ordered. 'You'll be surprised how much difference it makes to have the wind at your back.'

It was reassurance I'd received repeatedly at the Pole. Now that I was heading for the coast my route had reached its highest altitude and should, theoretically, start descending all the way to sea level. Even better, the winds that blow out from the centre of the continent would now be pushing me forward rather than gusting straight into my face as they had been. Still, I remained sceptical. How much faster could I realistically expect to ski? So far, the furthest I had skied on a single day was sixteen nautical miles and that was with a near-empty sledge in great conditions and perfect weather. I would need to equal this every single day for the next month to stand a chance of getting anywhere near the coast in time. By this reckoning, having completed only eleven nautical miles that day, I was already five nautical miles behind schedule. The numbers simply didn't work out.

'It's likely that we might be able to squeeze a few extra days out of the season,' Steve had said when I asked about the date of the deadline but he wouldn't be drawn into a specific promise.

For extra time to be of any use, I calculated, I would need at least ten days. I doubted this was what Steve had in mind.

Inside my tent the heat of the sun was so strong that I sat in only my thermals and opened the door wide to let in some cooling air. The view through the door as I sat cross-legged next to the stove made me sigh deeply and stare. Distant clouds sat like coils of wire on the horizon and refracted the sunlight so that they shimmered with the iridescence of oil on water. The snow beneath was brindled with the irregular shadows of shallow sastrugi. Sucking at a gloopy coffee fortified with protein powder, gazing at the achingly serene landscape framed by my tent door, I tried to imagine what it would feel like to return home without having crossed Antarctica. The thought of failure wasn't an easy one. I had never set out on an expedition and not returned successful to some degree. On a personal level, one of the main reasons I had wanted to cross Antarctica alone was to find out where my limits lay. If I failed because I had found those limits by being unable to continue for mental or physical reasons I would, at least, be returning home with some kind of answer. To fail because I had run out of time was a failure by logistics and as such, answered nothing. I would be left with the same question I had arrived with and that would be the bitter pill, the true failure. I couldn't imagine ever wanting to repeat this journey and so the question would likely always remain unanswered. This was my one and only opportunity and it would be wasted.

My mind floated northward beyond the horizon I could see, over the degrees and the miles that I had watched so memorably from the air. My thoughts rested on the Thiel Mountains that were less than five degrees of latitude away (thinking in degrees of latitude was more manageable than thinking in miles, kilometres or even days – the numbers were smaller). I could picture the flat-topped profile of the mountain range, the caps of ice sitting on squat buttes looking like elevated islands, each cap forming a lost world of white protected by the dark foundations of the sheer rock faces below. I felt a desire to see those mountains again, to touch a point of commonality with my outward journey. I wanted to feel that a circle had been completed and to enjoy the satisfaction of a circuit, even if it was not the one I had planned. A new resolution took shape in my head. I would give my all to every single day and see how far I could get before the plane came to find me in the days leading up to 26 January. If I was strict with my routines – getting out of the tent promptly in the mornings, keeping my breaks brief and efficient, skiing for the maximum number of hours while still allowing time for decent sleep – I considered it a good chance that I would see Thiel Mountains before I saw the plane. As I flew away from the ice I would need to know that there wasn't any more I could have done, that I had got as far across Antarctica as I possibly could. That was my covenant to myself.

To seal the pact I fetched the pot of peanut butter from my sledge and scooped a large spoonful so that the creamy paste crinkled into a thick heap of pleasure. A generous spoonful was to be my daily ration so that the pot lasted for as long as possible. I ate the peanut butter like ice cream, delighting in the salty sweetness of it. Sitting snug in my sun-warmed tent, looking out at a mesmerising view, alone in one of the remotest of places, it seemed that to leave this place of wonder sooner than I had to would be a sacrilege. Being alone again didn't feel as awful as I had feared; I didn't dare allow myself even to think it for fear of a jinx, but I might have even said that I was feeling comfortable with the isolation. I was in what I consider to be my spiritual home on the journey of my life. If I ever needed to summon the best of me it was now and in the days and weeks ahead. As I waited for sleep in my down nest

I promised myself not to stop until I saw the plane emerge in the sky – a sight I realised that I simultaneously both longed for and dreaded.

CHAPTER SIX

BALD-HEADED MEN

@felicity_aston Being alone again doesn't feel as bad as I feared. Helps that the sun is heating my tent nicely. Costa Del Pole!

@felicity_aston The sky is blue, the sun is shining. A really positive morning – not even porridge can bring me down.

This wasn't my first hallucination.

During an expedition across the Greenland ice sheet I had at times been struck by the distinct impression that I was skiing through a valley of long grass waving hypnotically in the breeze. Before that, while sleep-deprived at the end of an intense fortnight of skiing across the Canadian Arctic, I had heard my name called distinctly and repeatedly over the rush of the wind. When I turned to my team-mates skiing in line behind me, it was clear that neither of them had spoken. Later during the same trip, an Inuit guide told me that this was a common phenomenon on the sea ice of the far north and that it was the voice of spirits.

'The ancestors say that you must never answer the spirits when they call your name,' he said in a quiet, serious voice.

Another, less poetic, explanation is that my brain, starved of data by the white noise of the constant wind, was simply filling in the gaps – an auditory hallucination. To avoid a repeat of these experiences while I was alone, the sport psychologist Dr Pack had suggested in one of our pre-expedition conversations that I use mental imagery to provide the stimulus my brain craved. I was to spend time mentally recalling scenes I knew well, such as a room of my flat or scenes from a journey I made regularly. He advised me that the trick was to make the images as vivid as possible by enhancing the colours and the detail, remembering each and every element of the scene one by one to recreate the whole, like assembling a high resolution photograph one pixel at a time. By providing my brain with so much virtual stimulus the theory was that it would be prevented from noticing the lack of real material in the polar landscape around me. If my brain didn't notice the blanks it would hopefully be prevented from creating 'fill-in' perceptions and I wouldn't have any hallucinations of any variety.

When Dr Pack explained all this to me I remember an awkward pause, as if there was something that he hesitated to ask.

'If, after using the imagery technique, you still had hallucinations, what would be really interesting is to see whether the subject of the imagery you use affects them,' he admitted. 'For example, if you consistently recalled images of penguins, would you start to experience penguin-related hallucinations?'

After a lengthy discussion we agreed that I would attempt to use imagery of seaside scenes from around my home in Kent that I knew well and, if I still experienced hallucinations, to note whether they took on a particularly coastal theme.

And so it was that as I skied towards Christmas morning on the polar plateau of Antarctica, the impact of my first hallucinatory experience of the expedition was slightly tempered by the disappointment that it had nothing to do with the sea. As I ploughed dizzily through the same kind of dense disorientating whiteout that had become such a regular feature of my journey I was surprisingly calm to notice a small man emerge from a hiding place (that I assumed was probably a large sastrugi hidden in the flat light) on my right. He was only a few feet high with a round, bald head and triangular body. It was clearly a vision, the figure was transparent and etched in grey so that it was barely perceptible against the close weather and yet it was real enough for me to see details of the figure's expression and body language. I was left in no doubt that I had clumsily blundered into this little man's world and that my disturbance had forced him unwillingly from his hiding place. He looked both annoyed and a little embarrassed to be startled into the open, hurriedly scurried off into the blizzard, and was gone. A short while later I saw another figure. He was of a comparable size and stature to the first character and similarly emerged from behind an unseen sastrugi, but this time the vision rode a tiny dinosaur, a bonsai triceratops. Bolder and more belligerent than the first little man, he shook his fist at me for intruding into his personal space before galloping off into the haze on his Cretaceous charger.

Several times during the day I saw hands with one single outstretched, pointing, finger and frilly cuffs at the wrist that looked exactly like the illustrations sometimes used as bullet points to emphasise lines of text. The hands, completely disembodied from any other anatomy, floated at eye level and urgently prodded the air ahead to show me the way. Occasionally the hands appeared as applauding pairs, hovering to one side to give the impression of supportive spectators. In retrospect it seems bizarre that these inchoate hallucinations didn't cause me to worry or even pause in my pace. I registered the fact that I'd just seen little men running around Antarctica (with and without dinosaurs) and I replayed the visions in my mind as I skied on but the incidents didn't feel at all remarkable. I had become so accustomed to the fact that the world I travelled through didn't obey any of the normal rules of experience that the hallucinations took on as much significance as the sensation of floating when I slept, sastrugi transformed by mirage into mountains, or the falling of snowflakes from a blue sky. So many things about my journey made my mind boggle that it seemed easier not to think too hard about any of them. Even the normal division of day and night couldn't be relied upon. The day I skied through had begun long before I arrived on the continent and wouldn't end until long after I had left. (The first sunset in Antarctica would occur sometime in February.)

My only point of curiosity about the hallucinations was why they had occurred now. I had been through worse weather that had deprived me of my sense of place for longer. Perhaps it was down to my level of exhaustion. Or maybe a reflection of my desire for company – though in many ways I felt less alone now. Firstly, I was no longer on the 'wrong side' of Antarctica which meant that help would be just a little bit closer should

I need it. Secondly, while at the Pole, someone had mentioned that there were over 9,000 people following the messages I sent from my satellite phone through to Twitter. I was astounded. On leaving the UK a few months before, the figure had been little more than 400. The next time I picked up the satellite phone to laboriously type in a message to the expedition Twitter account, the thought of the number of people reading them made me pause, as if struck by cyber stage fright. Until now, Twitter had been a form of comfort in that it provided a way to record what was happening to me. It ensured that my existence was registered somewhere, a link, however tenuous, with the outside world. Now that I knew so many people were following, the link took on more substance. Even though I wasn't able to see any of the comments, replies or retweets, just the knowledge that people I had never met in parts of the world I had never seen were watching, caring and willing me on had a huge impact. They seemed to fill the tent with their presence so that I didn't feel quite so alone. It provided proof that I wasn't beyond the reach of the human family after all but was still connected to the larger social tribe. I noticed that the satellite phone was the first thing I reached for when I crawled into the tent – even before I had removed my boots or jacket – and that I sat with the handset permanently nestled in my lap like a child's comforter. It was undoubtedly the piece of equipment most precious to me, above even the stove or my sleeping bag, because just as my tent was a safety net against the cold, the satellite phone was a safety net against my alone-ness and I found the isolation far more terrifying than the temperature.

On Christmas Day the sun finally reappeared as a hard-edged disc in the sky behind the layers of cloud, as harmless to gaze at as the moon. It gave no texture to the snow surface below it but provided a point of reference in my otherwise seemingly dimensionless surroundings. I stumbled blindly forwards through a hidden landscape, my skis slipping and twisting under my feet as I pushed them over invisible sastrugi. The turbulent wind worked with cunning to knock me off balance, the force of the gusts pushing me roughly from one direction then another so that I moved clumsily in a series of lurches rather than a continuous flow. I could feel the heavy resistance of my sledges ploughing through soft snow behind me and the reluctance of different muscles and joints in turn as my body blundered mechanically onwards. My knees in particular grumbled at the extra punishment. I skied with only one ski pole because in my other hand I clasped a compass which hung around my neck on a long cord. I held it out in front of me, flat on the palm of my mitt, so that I could keep my eyes glued to the needle as I moved. That morning, as always, I had used my GPS to find the correct direction of travel and dialled the heading into my compass, turning off the GPS immediately afterwards to conserve the batteries. In bad weather I was forced to ski with my head bowed to watch the compass, adjusting the direction of my skis with every stride to match each twitch of the needle in order not to veer off course. Without a horizon or any distinguishable feature to use as a guide, if I lifted my eyes from the needle for so much as a few paces I would find that I had immediately swerved from my heading – even though I could swear I had done nothing but slide one ski directly in front of the other. It has always struck me as odd that the body apparently has no instinctive ability to move in a straight line.

Now that the sun had reappeared, no matter how faintly, it provided a fixed point that I could navigate by without needing to look at my compass so often. All day I lunged through the thick weather toward the sun, my eyes fixed on what was sometimes no more than a barely perceptible white glow behind dirty, cotton wool clouds, like the remnants of a tiny ember buried deep within a long-dead fire. I watched nervously as the smoky cloud repeatedly thickened around my guiding light, threatening to blot it from view completely. Each time the sun faded from sight my mental muscles tensed in dread that it had gone for good and yet I would march forward in stubborn belief that the light would return – and it always did. No matter how thick the cloud became, the sun would fight its way through even if only as the slightest of glimmers. It seemed that my desperation to keep sight of the sun was matched by the determination of the sun to get at least a scintilla of light through to me. It was as if it understood that I needed the physical connection, a sightline between us to give me the impetus to keep going, a representation of hope that I clung to pathetically. I imagined the sun battling to find a way through the weather, prising apart the clouds with its immense strength just to let me know that it was still there, to give me faith that the weather was only temporary, to make sure I knew I wasn't abandoned.

By the time I had skied for a dozen hours the sun had completed half a circuit around the sky, moving from a place away to my right, across the space in front of me, to a position on my left. In my last hour it broke through the weather as a silver flame. The pale disc I'd seen occasionally through a veil of cloud was now totally transmuted into a cruciform flare as dense as white-hot steel. A leaden sky above a bleak landscape of ashen snow should have felt sombre but the silver light of the sun gave Antarctica a seasonal feel. Something of the magic of Christmas fell over everything so that it seemed more peaceful although nothing but the light had changed. The wind still swirled around me throwing snow into the air but now it felt as if the weather simply slid over my protective shell of windproof clothing. The sun looked like a nativity star and I was filled with certainty that it was watching over me, a guardian, a protector, a lucky omen. I wasn't alone and I felt incredibly blessed to have such an inspiring companion.

Having pitched my tent I lingered outside for a moment, reluctant to let my guiding star out of sight, hesitating to bring the magic of the last few hours to an end. Sure enough as I ducked into my shelter the spell was broken. The tent rattled in the wind and the air outside whined mournfully as it squeezed through the guy ropes. Weak sunlight filtered through the green fabric of the Hilleberg creating a blue wash. It seemed to suck the colour out of everything and made me feel cold. I lit the stove, took off my icy outer clothing and sat in the down folds of my sleeping bag. This was usually enough to shake off the frigidness of the ski but today, I still felt chilled.

I could picture exactly what my family would be doing at that moment to celebrate Christmas Day and it contrasted sharply with my solitary tent lost in the vastness of the Antarctic plateau. My Christmas dinner was a freeze-dried spaghetti bolognaise. Two years before I had been in a similar spot not far away, sharing a tent with the team and eating freeze-dried chicken tikka masala as my festive meal. With the season falling half way through the busy austral summer, I had enjoyed plenty of guaranteed white Christmases in Antarctica over the years. This was to be the third in a row I had spent near the South Pole but it was the very first I had ever spent alone.

Lying in my sleeping bag but unable to sleep I reached for my camera and took a picture of myself. I don't know why, perhaps it was an attempt to mark the day as different; taking pictures as an act of ritual or ceremony rather than as a simple matter of record. Looking at my self-portrait I was surprised to see how I felt on the inside so accurately portrayed in my face. I looked exactly as I felt; worn and fragile, my features heavy with exposure to the cold, my hair as wild as Medusa after being stowed under a hat for more than a month. My skin was unmarked but the tinted light of the tent made me look unhealthily wan. I looked into my own eyes curiously, trying to assess what they told me, and decided that I was tested but not beaten. There was still intensity in my glare at the camera lens.

Out of habit I reached for the locket around my neck and held it in the palm of my fist but I avoided opening it to look at the family picture inside because I knew it would only make those smiling faces feel further away. As it was I seemed unable to stop the cold and isolation around me seeping into my thoughts and for the first time since leaving the Pole I gave in to the emotion and allowed myself to cry.

The simple pleasures of my day-to-day life back home seemed so far from my present reality that it felt barely possible they could be real and not some vision of an imagined paradise. The thought of curling up with a loved one on a sofa somewhere warm with a glass of wine appeared to me then to be the greatest luxury I could ask for from life – and the fact that at home it was possible to experience such comfort on demand struck me as the most exulted achievement of mankind. To be free to experience such simple pleasure is a privilege I am guilty of too often taking for granted. Over the last decade my life has been almost exclusively pre-occupied by the desire for adventure, my mind relentlessly buzzing with plans for future journeys. And yet, as soon as my wish to disappear over the horizon into some remote corner of the planet is granted, my mind clings onto all the sentimental details of home and I find that my daydreams of escaping across wide open spaces are replaced not just by precious recollections of moments of affection with a loved one but by fond memories of family gatherings, jokes shared with siblings and time with friends.

Expeditions temporarily empty my life of all but the basic concerns of eating, sleeping, travel and staying safe. Like clearing undergrowth from a garden to discover the outline of borders and flowerbeds underneath, reducing life to just the essentials reveals the fundamental structure that underpins the whole. I found that, with life at its most basic and my spirit stretched, what was most dear to me was memories of time spent with those I love. I take this as a clear indication that, above all else, this is what is important in my life. It was a lesson I had been taught before, but a lesson I needed to learn again. It was a lesson I needed to remember.

Months after returning home, a priest in Italy sent me his thoughts on Antarctica. He wrote of his belief that 'everything must be stripped away in order to truly hear again'. The phrase filled me with emotion because it expressed precisely something I had felt deeply in Antarctica. It is a place that strips away all but the essential and what is left is what is most important. It enables a clarity of thought only possible when we are at our rawest and most genuine – when we are scared, lonely, exposed. What is more, the lack of any physical distraction and the purity of the landscape allows the important questions to float to the surface, allows us the space, freedom and clarity to ponder our purpose and our place in the scheme of things.

Returning home from a trip can be difficult; there is, inevitably, a sense of anti-climax. Many people fill the hole left by a past adventure by planning another trip or seeking the next escape. I'm wary of doing the same, worried that it could become a negative spiral, that I would become so intent on adventure that I would lose the ability to be content at home. Instead, I am determined that the two big pulls on my life, adventure and home, should provide me with balance rather than conflict. I cannot envision a future for myself without travel and adventure but expeditions also teach me to value the pleasures of everyday life. When tempted to moan about the annoyances of a crowded supermarket, I remind myself of how incredible the thought of wandering around a place stocked with every food imaginable appeared to me when tucking into repetitive rations in a tent. If I find myself less than enthusiastic about travelling to a family event, I reminisce about how much I would have given for such a pleasure when in the wilderness. The same process works in reverse; when feeling sorry for myself in a cold tent I made sure to recollect that I was living my dream. I believe the two halves of my life can complement each other and work in harmony; expeditions teach me to appreciate the blessings of home; and home reinforces the value of adventures.

Turning off the camera I slipped out the battery and tucked it down my front where it lived in my sports-top alongside a lighter, MP3 player and satellite phone power pack. Bracing myself against the burn of cold material I thrust my feet to the very bottom of my sleeping bag, awkwardly twisting the rest of my body into place. Fastening the zip, I reached for the metal fuel bottle that was normally attached to my stove. The bottle was empty but the pump, which pressurises the liquid fuel so that it can be burnt as a gas, had become jammed in the narrow screwneck. I couldn't refill the bottle, and therefore couldn't use my stove, until I removed the pump. I hoped that warming the bottle in my sleeping bag overnight might allow me to loosen the pump in the morning but I winced at the touch of the cold metal bottle which burned like white heat as I tucked it between my knees, even though it was wrapped in a fleece jacket. The sickly smell of stove fuel floated upward through the folds of my sleeping bag – a smell that I suspected would linger in the material forever as a result. Afraid of oversleeping and losing valuable ski time, I tucked my tiny alarm in the folds of my hat that I wore to sleep near my left ear so that I would be able to hear it clearly. I'd discovered that unless the alarm was close to my ear, the sound would get lost in the volume of a sleeping bag.

As I lay still, waiting for my body heat to warm the insulated space around me, all the extra objects I slept with to keep them from freezing made me feel penned in. It was important that I didn't move around too much in my sleep in case I damaged any of the equipment tucked around my body. As a result even the most natural sleeping position felt a little contrived. Lying tensely on the floor of the tent trying to block out the lonesome sound of the wind and not to fidget, I was tormented by memories of sleeping with nothing but a duvet pulled over me, of having space to move arms and legs as I pleased, the freedom of a mattress...

No sooner had I opened my eyes than I reached for the door zip to check the weather. I felt a surge of relief; I could see blue. Even better, when I fished the fuel bottle from the depths of my sleeping bag the pump gave with an easy twist and was free.

A few hours later when I finally emerged from the cramped tent and stretched upright I lifted my face to the sun, which radiated so brightly that I could feel its warmth on my skin.

'Good Morning!' I bellowed to the sky as had become my habit on sunny days.

It seemed that the sun's rays gleamed even brighter for my enthusiasm. I squinted upwards to watch the pulsating circle of white and noticed rainbow spikes protruding outward from the star so far that they almost seemed to touch the ground. The sun was reaching for me – a celestial hug.

Looking north I ran my sight over the endless plain ahead. The sun threw dark and precise shadows from each lump and imperfection of the snow surface so that every detail stood out clearly. The smooth white void of the day before had been dramatically transformed into a calloused crust of intricate texture. My heart thumped in grim determination as I contemplated it. The irregular terrain would be hard work to ski over, particularly with my odd gait thanks to the dodgy ski, but with the sun in the sky I could at least see every obstacle, making it easier to avoid the worst. These were the best weather conditions I'd had in a week and I knew I had to make the most of them. As I packed away the tent in my sledge my brain fizzed with calculations, working out how many miles I'd need to cover in order to make up for the disappointing progress of the last few days. I felt invigorated by the challenge of a new target and a fresh sense of urgency. The distance I had in mind was ambitious but as I clipped the toes of my boots into the ski bindings I was excited to be launching myself toward the horizon. I paused only to glance behind me to scan my recent campsite for any forgotten belongings and to call out thanks to the ground for my stay as I did every morning. I pulled my goggles into place while already on the move, feeling the strength in my stride. It seemed incredible that a body which had felt so sore and broken just twelve hours previously could now be so compliant.

Rather than skiing with one ski pole, head bowed to watch the needle of my compass, in the better weather I was able to fix my gaze on a prominent patch of shade on the horizon and ski towards it. When I drew near to my marker I would simply choose another distant patch of shade directly ahead and in that way keep myself on a straight heading north. I could feel the difference in my pace as a result, satisfied that the rough snow under my skis seemed to be flying by beneath me. It seemed that the faster I skied, the greater my desire to push even harder – and the harder I drove myself the stronger I felt. The sensation was close to euphoric.

Usually my attention was focused exclusively on the patch of shade I had chosen to head for. I was careful not to let my sight wander but occasionally I would risk an upwards glance at the sun. It was not a perfectly clear sky but veined with a web of thin, high cloud and I worried it might thicken. Over time the intense indigo of the morning sky faded into a baby blue and the shadows that had been so sharp began to soften, but each time I nervously peered skyward, the sun seemed to beam reassurance at me.

'No matter how bad the weather gets,' I imagined it saying, 'I will not leave you today.'

As if to reinforce the point, a wide band of white light encircled the sun, a halo caused by the refraction of light in the gathering cloud. No matter how fast or how slow I travelled, the sun and its colourless, circular rainbow glided beside me, effortlessly keeping pace. The wind still blew in my face and the snow still seemed to suck at my skis and sledge just as it had done the day before, but every time I felt myself dwelling on the effort of each stride I'd turn my face to the sun and send silent thanks, reminding myself how much worse it could be. The act took on the significance of a superstition, as if a failure to demonstrate my gratitude might hasten a turn in the weather.

Searching the horizon for another marker to aim for, my eyes picked out a dark dot practically straight ahead. I was struck by a vague impression that this dot was different in some way, that it was peculiarly distinct – even though I had no idea why. This dot was no larger and no darker than any other shadow on the landscape so I ignored the thought and yet each time I allowed the dot to slide from my gaze, my eyes would effortlessly pick out the same spot when I rescanned the horizon. Over time I became convinced that it wasn't the shadow of a large sastrugi but an object on the ice. It might be an overlooked flag left behind by a science field party, or a marker placed by an expedition to make a depot more visible. As I drew closer the dot seemed too big to be a flag. I began to wonder if it might be a cluster of fuel barrels. Whatever it was, it made a great navigational aid. Knowing I had such a reliable feature to aim for I could loosen my focus and allow myself to glance around, gazing in wonder at the white halo which still circled the sun and which became ever clearer as a silky veil thickened over the blue.

I felt a slow drop in temperature as the intensity of the sun was weakened by the gathering cloud and I noticed that my view of the object up ahead began to shimmer as if in a heat haze. My brain became pre-occupied in trying to understand the physics behind this development, my sluggish synapses dragging half-remembered science from deep in my memory. As I contemplated what I was seeing, I noticed something else. I held back my excitement for a moment while I squinted hard into the distance to try and be sure that I wasn't mistaken. It was not one object up ahead, but two – and it wasn't the shimmer of heat haze I could see but movement. The object, or objects, were moving!

My mind scrambled for an explanation. Could it be people? I rejected the idea instantly. Although I was aware that there were other expeditions out here on the plateau heading for the South Pole, in a continent larger than the United States of America and Mexico combined it was highly unlikely that I would bump into any of them. Having experienced the trickery of Antarctica before, I felt sure that this mystery would be resolved by a disappointingly mundane explanation. Even so, I watched the dark shapes closely. Without any sense of scale in the landscape around me it was impossible to guess accurately how close I was and even though my curiosity was heightened to the point that it made me itch, there was nothing I could do but plod slowly onward towards the cryptic blobs. At times I was convinced it was two objects moving independently while at others I resigned myself sadly to the fact that this was no more than two clusters of flags blowing in the wind.

After hours of hovering tantalisingly beyond identification, the mysterious objects suddenly, within what felt like a matter of seconds, drew immediately near.

There was now no doubt. The two objects were people – and they were skiing towards me.

What was the etiquette for such a situation? For a brief moment I wondered if I should ski dramatically to the right or left in order to avoid the approaching duo – then I realised that

I wouldn't have got far enough by the time we were upon each other to wave gracefully from a distance. I laughed at myself. Here I was in the emptiest wilderness on Earth, having not seen another living being for a week, plotting how to circumvent meeting the last humans I was likely to see in a month or more. It was taking my British reserve to new extremes. I stopped and hurriedly wiped the frozen snot, dribble and condensed breath from the outside of my mask, even squeezing a gloved finger beneath the ice-hard material to check I didn't have the remnants of chocolate and snacks all over my face. By the time I looked up, the two skiers were so close that I could pick out the names printed on the front of their jackets; 'Cas' and 'Jonesy'. I knew immediately who they were. We'd never met but I'd heard of two Australian adventurers who had set out for the South Pole from the same coast I was now heading for myself.

'Hello!' one of them bellowed from a distance.

'Hello!' I shouted back as a huge, excited grin spread across my face under my mask.

When we drew close there were no introductions. I threw my arms around them both and they seemed just as enthusiastic to see me. They each towed enormous sledges which I noticed were almost empty and although both wore goggles and face masks, from the skin that was visible I could see that they had been exposed to Antarctica for a long time. As Cas spoke, the sores on his badly chapped lips broke open and started to bleed. Jonesy's nose was frostbitten at the tip and I noticed that condensed moisture had frozen over the scabs forming a small icicle. They were both in good spirits despite being obviously exhausted and it felt like a meeting of old friends rather than a chance encounter with strangers. They were eager for news of the Pole.

'Is it like this all the way?' Cas asked, nodding toward the ground.

I thought about it for a second. For much of the last week I hadn't been able to see the ground.

'It certainly doesn't get any worse,' I answered.

They told me of horrendous weather at the coast which had left them snowbound in their tent for a week, of wading through deep drifts left behind by the storms and of rough terrain in the eighty-seventh degree. We spoke rapidly to each other, partly due to the novelty of conversation but also because the longer we stood speaking the colder we got. More importantly we were each on a schedule. They had their mileage target for the day just as I did, and wasted minutes meant lost miles. We wished each other well and after another round of enthusiastic hugs, I headed northwards and they continued south. A few minutes later, I looked around to see that they had already become two dark and indistinct blurs made small by the vastness around them. I noted that they skied side-by-side and wondered if they would be talking to each other about our meeting or skiing along in silence, each digesting the new information about their onward journey. For a brief moment I was struck with intense sadness. I had no one to share my thoughts with, no one with whom to relive the excitement of probably the most bizarre meeting of my life. For those few moments I had been reminded of the reassurance that comes with being able to share an experience. Once more, I saw clearly that the absence of a companion did more than simply add isolation to the challenges of a polar journey – it heightened the fear, the doubt and anxiety, sharpened the emotional stress. I envied Cas and Jonesy their companionship in this most lonely of places.

I felt disapproval from the sky.

'Of course, I have you as a wonderful companion,' I mentally transmitted to the sun to quickly redeem myself.

Occasionally as I skied I would conjure companions from my memories of previous expeditions, imagining characters I had travelled with in the past to be skiing alongside me, guessing what jokes or conversation we would share. Sometimes I would invent new teams out of friends who had never met each other and tried to predict whether or not they would get along. My imaginary companions never appeared physically as hallucinations but as I skied I told myself that I was simply taking a turn at navigating from the front and that if I turned around they would all be there in single file behind me. This self-deception was particularly useful at break times. The demon voices that plagued me every morning would return every time I stopped skiing, filling my head with convincing and persuasive reasons why it was not only a good idea, but bordering on imperative, that I call it a day and pitch my tent. The thought of crawling into the shelter of the Hilleberg, of escaping the wind and the cold, of being able to slide into my waiting sleeping bag was as alluring as the wafting aroma of freshly ground coffee. I resisted the urge by trying to think as a leader rather than allowing myself to sink into the emotional quagmire of my alone-ness. I made decisions for my imaginary group rather than as an individual and told myself that there would now be witnesses to any capitulation into apathy. It was a complex self-deception but it seemed to work.

A team generates a bubble of security around itself even though the physical hazards themselves don't change, in much the same way that everyone tends to feel safer when travelling in a group even though the reality may be that they are just as vulnerable as when travelling alone. If I'd had real companions I'm sure that Antarctica would have appeared less daunting and the challenges of life on the ice more manageable. The knowledge that any relapse into bad behaviour wouldn't be observed made self-discipline all the more difficult. I was acutely aware of the fact that ever since the plane had first left me alone on the Ross Ice Shelf I had been far more emotionally indulgent with myself than on any other expedition. If I felt upset I cried, if I was annoyed with myself I got visibly angry. I allowed my inner emotions to flow into outward expression because there was no one to witness my outbursts. I had cried far more during this journey than on any other simply because there was no one to witness it – but then, perhaps, nothing would have felt so desperate if I had had a companion.

I had known that the good weather wouldn't last forever, that the sun could only protect me for so long, but even so as I emerged from my tent the following morning I couldn't help but feel deflated. The contrast had faded almost to nothing.

'But you promised!' I whined at the sky, remembering the assurances from the sun the previous day.

I heard a thought in my head that didn't feel like my own. 'I promised I wouldn't leave you all day – and I didn't. Today is a new day.'

Grudgingly I had to concede that, strictly speaking, the promise had been day specific. I struck camp in a sulk, dreading the mind-numbing hours of stumbling and frustration that I knew were ahead of me. It didn't seem fair to allow me a glimpse of what could be, only to bury it in cloud once again.

'What did you expect from Antarctica?' came the same voice-like thought.

I ignored it, refusing in my petulant state to respond. With my sledges packed and ski bindings fastened securely in place I squared up to the unseen horizon like a sprinter at the start line of a race. I felt my face set beneath my mask and my mind fall into neutral to block out the seductive voices of inertia that lurked endlessly in my headspace. I pushed forward and registered the familiar stretch of muscle, clocking in each ache and pain as it made itself felt in turn: a smarting from my toe where it had become sore under the crease of my ski boot; the incessant jab of my trapezoid with each movement of my ski pole; the quiet, continuous discomfort of the strain in my elbow; the urgent complaint from each of my knees (today louder from my left than my right); the soft burn of my fist clenched within my mitt; the abrasive friction of my harness against the tender bruising on my hips; the sting of cold air being drawn through lips already raw with exposure; the heat of the spiralling pressure along my shin caused by my misaligned ski binding. A dozen minor discomforts harmonised into a singular note of annoyance.

As a child I was always fascinated by the fact that focusing intently on a single word, repeating it over and over, eventually renders it meaningless. Now, I concentrated intently on each discomfort in turn, breaking it down until it became nothing more than a sensation. The aches and pains didn't go away but I found that with concentrated mental effort I could at least relegate them to a kind of general background noise of irritation.

There was just enough light to be able to navigate by sight using the merest hints of shadow on the snow as markers. In the shifting light I had to focus intently on each marker then pause when I reached it, squinting into the blanched gloom to detect any slight patch of imperfection in the greyish white ground ahead to aim for. As the visibility steadily worsened, the distance between the markers got shorter until I was moving between patches of shade no more than a few metres apart. Halfway through the day, peering into the murk for my next marker, I noticed a pale blue eye peering at me from the blankness. Then, as if they were materialising out of nothing, I could see them everywhere, all around me: the centres of sastrugi, identical in form to the barrel of a wave. What scared me was the size of them. When I had come across such eyes before, they had been the size of a fist but those ahead of me now were larger than shopping trolleys. To create eyes this big I knew the sastrugi around them had to be huge but I couldn't see the snow formations themselves, just the blue shadows of the spaces created beneath and within them as the waves of hard-packed, wind-sculpted snow curled over themselves like the white-horses of the sea. I skied forward a few paces and noticed a huge blue void a few feet to my left. It was big enough to fall into and deep enough that if I did fall I could easily sprain, strain or break something. Distracted by the void I didn't immediately notice the open pit directly in my path ahead until my ski-tips were already over hanging the lip of the huge powder-blue hole.

I stopped to look around me with new anxiety. The surrounding snow seemed full of fresh menace. Awkwardly I manoeuvred my skis to the left of the blue space, waddling like a duck to haul my sledges over the uneven ground. As I worked my way around the rim of the dimly lit cavity I could make out thick tongues of hard-packed snow overhanging the hollow space. Each tongue was the size of a dolphin. I struggled to imagine how big these sastrugi must be given the disruption around me. It made me feel small and vulnerable, like Alice wandering in a nightmare wonderland.

I used the eyes of the sastrugi to navigate, skiing from one to the next, clambering and falling as I dragged my sledges over the rough ground I couldn't see. Often I'd have to stop and twist awkwardly on my skis to haul my sledges by hand or flick my skis lengthways across an incline, digging my edges into the snowpack for purchase and side-stepping upwards. At times I'd stand upright having yanked my sledges over an unseen formation of snow and had the distinct sensation of being surrounded by space, as if standing on a narrow pedestal. I didn't understand the landscape around me, unable to translate my sensations of the space into a mental image of what might be concealed in the whiteout. It was confusing and I didn't have the energy to work it out, I just needed to keep moving forward. At one point my skis slipped and I fell heavily onto my sledges. I tried to stand but with my knees and ankles twisted into awkward angles, freeing myself was going to take some thought. I lay motionless where I had fallen for a moment, resisting the urge to burst into tears of frustration. Drifting snow being blown along the ground by the wind poured over me and my sledges, small hard particles of ice gathering in the folds of my jacket and I wondered how long it would take before it would cover me completely, the drift building around and over me until I became a part of it.

Wearily I lifted myself onto my elbows and, working slowly, loosened the binding on each ski to release my feet before trudging wearily up the remaining incline, using the skis as walking poles.

Reaching the top I felt the wind blow against my body as I gazed northward for a second, the cold air freezing the hairs in my nose, making it twitch like a rabbit. Up ahead the light had changed. There was a dull yellow smudge on the grey sky like a nicotine stain. It was the sun, burning free of its concealment behind the cloud. My heart lurched in gratitude, my cheeks aching with a sudden, spontaneous grin. As I watched, the sky broke open and smoky beams of sunlight fell earthwards through translucent air filled with ice-mist and vapour. I sniffed back tears of relief, treating myself to a wipe of my running nose along the back of my mitt.

'Thank you, thank you, thank you,' I whispered aloud, the hiss of breath loud in my ears.

But as the sunlight lit the landscape my eyes grew wide in astonishment. Revealing itself as steadily from the gloom as a developing photograph was a black-and-white scene of devastation, a tortured terrain of buckled ground. The tallest sastrugi I had ever seen rose into ridges and towers like battlements. Squared blocks of hardened snow and sculpted ice rested on each other like the altars of giants and snow streamed between them, ushered by the wind, so that the ground seethed in restless movement. It felt like I had stumbled across the ruins of a great city from a past apocalypse. I felt dwarfed and subdued by the magnitude of it.

This must be the rough ground Cas and Jonesy talked about, I thought to myself. Rough ground was an understatement; I had never seen anything like it. The large spaces I had seen as deep blue pools in the dull flattened white of the bad visibility made sense now – they were all that was visible of the voids and dells between these icy monoliths. This is why the going had been so difficult. Scanning the tumultuous scene I despaired at finding a route through the debris, there didn't seem to be room to squeeze between one towering obstacle and the next without clambering in and out of the deep spaces formed like windscoops at their bases. I shivered but it wasn't the cold giving me goosebumps, rather the landscape. The dirty brown of the light, the otherworldly silhouettes of the enormous sastrugi and the foreboding I felt made the scene eerie. The terrain took on a nefarious aggression of its own, yet I responded by refusing to be daunted. I could feel my determination rising to meet the intimidation of the environment. I realised I was reaping the benefit of previous expedition experiences. I had laboured over arduous ground with sledges before and knew that despite the formidable appearance of the chaos ahead, there would be a way through it. This was the sort of challenge I had come to Antarctica better prepared to face and for once I felt like I was in familiar territory. I glanced upward at the now blinding light flooding through the cracks in the cloud. There was no audible promise but I could feel its reassurance. The sun would be with me every stumbling step of the way.

With care I alternately cajoled and yanked my two sledges over and around obstacle after obstacle. As much as possible I tried to keep to the high ground where the snow was firmer, blown solid by the pressure of the wind, but frequently the path of least resistance led me down into gulches where snow the consistency of silt gathered in drifts. Continuously climbing up and over the disrupted terrain was tiring but as I glanced at my watch and noticed that it was time to camp I had to admit that I was enjoying myself. The sun had held its place in the sky and the mammoth sastrugi, despite being intimidating, were undeniably impressive. I felt as if I had spent the afternoon clambering through a closely packed sculpture park. Some of the blocks of wind-packed snow had sides so smooth that I could run my gloved fingers along their surfaces, leaving deep grooves in the fine sand-like crystals. The shades of blue in the folds of opaque ice were so delicate and fragile that it made me ache with desire to preserve or record them in some way. I tried to take a picture but even as I did so I knew the digital echo would be a far cry from the real thing. Nature is shrewd at creating perfection that is thoroughly beyond our ability to capture or replicate.

I skied later than usual in an attempt to find somewhere flat enough for the Hilleberg. I thought I'd found the perfect spot but as I crawled in through the door on hands and knees I caught sight of the ground sheet pulled in ruches by an odd tension. When I flopped outstretched onto it I could see why. What had appeared to be a flat patch of ground was in fact a large hump. Even worse, a stubborn shelf of rock hard snow that had somehow escaped my close inspection of the site bulged into the left side of the space. I decided I didn't have the energy to move camp but as I pulled on my sleeping bag that evening I found myself weighing up the merits of sleeping with a lump in my back versus lying pressed up against the wall of the tent curled around a cold incline. While considering each of the equally unappealing choices the Hilleberg was lit by a golden glow, as if the headlights of a passing car had pierced the darkness. I smiled to myself: the sun had broken through the cloud and would be waiting for me in the morning.

CHAPTER SEVEN

SUNDOGS AND HALOES

@felicity_aston When the sun reappears it feels like a miracle and nothing seems quite as bad as it did before.

@felicity_aston One of those days that makes you thank your lucky stars to be in Antarctica. Everything was sparkling.

@felicity_aston Disaster. I've reached the bottom of my pot of peanut butter.

There was something different about my view. Usually the horizon feels close, on the flat it is perhaps three or four nautical miles away, but now it seemed much further. As I narrowed my eyes to peer into the distance I was struck with the impression that I could see all the way to the ocean. It felt like a view of a thousand kilometres. I stood still for a while and recognised the thump of my heart and the tingling in my blood stream – it was a sense of intimidation. The sudden visualisation of just how far I still had to go was frightening. The wind blew against my back and scraped along the side of my hood, filling my ears with its constant fricative. Low ridges of sastrugi twisted away from me like the braided streams of an intricate river delta, channelling the drifting snow which was sent tumbling northwards by the wind at a speed I envied. Each particle span gracefully over the hardened surface, a surface I knew would feel as cold and firm to the touch as wet stone. With distance, the long interlacing ridge-lines of the sastrugi appeared to shorten and form a tighter weave until the alternating light and dark of closely packed ridge and trough beneath the horizon resembled the minute overlapping scales of a silver fish. Further away still, the pattern changed again, becoming more foliose, like the minute flaky gradations of lichen. Nothing was white or blue, everything had a shade to it: mauve, celadon, blush, amber, peach. Even the sallow sky, striped with half-hearted washes of cloud, glimmered with flecks of colour like the skin of a freshwater pearl. The sun hid itself behind an outcrop of dim, dense cloud, setting the edges alight with magnesium fire. As I took it all in, gentle but insistent fingers of cold probed my layers of clothing, their tingling touch filtering inwards as if each material layer I wore was steadily dissolved by degrees into nothing more protective than a loose webbing of fibres. I felt the cold coming but still I stood motionless, letting the imprint of the view sink into me as surely as the chill.

It's impossible to witness such a landscape and not be struck by just how vast and how empty the southern continent truly is. In England every stone, every clump of soil, has been touched by repeated human hands through endless ages. The land itself is inlaid with the human story and you can sense those histories as you pass through it, the scenery dense with echoes of past times. Successive generations have physically shaped the land; levelling hilltops, digging dykes, cutting pathways through mountains, so that the past of a region, as well as the life of those who live in its present, is recorded in its topography. When I first travelled to Canada, particularly the far north-east coasts of Labrador, I felt unnerved by the wilderness there. It took me a while to realise that it was the absence of that dense human history soaked into the soil and rock that unsettled me. It felt as if humans were only lightly grafted onto the surface of those wild places and that we could be shrugged away at any time.

Antarctica takes this impression to its extreme. Humans have been crossing the Antarctic plateau intermittently for a century but our tracks and footprints have been blown clean. Any flags or markers left behind have been vibrated by storms into ragged splinters. Even the few stations and refuges built on that immense raised interior of the continent have silted over as soon as our backs are turned, successive layers of dust-like snow covering over the blemish until it is pushed beneath the surface, encased unseen within the ice. Mankind, for the moment, has not managed to take root here and the only indelible mark is a diluted chemical signature in the ice – the result of radiation and pollution carried south on the wind.

A hundred years after its first human visitors, the plateau is not over-run with scientists or explorers. I had met people on my transect but only because the polar community tends to confine itself to invisible pathways, led by the common numbers in our GPS units, and most usually converging on the Pole. Livestock in a field seem at first glance to be roaming wherever they please but an image of their grazing areas from the air reveals well-trodden paths, radiating in erratic lines from a common spot, proving that the movement is actually very repetitive and limited. If all the tracks made by travel in Antarctica over the years were visible, I imagine an aerial image would resemble those pictures of fields with systematic pathways radiating from the Pole. It is rare that any expedition veers too far from these known but unseen trails. There are still immense tracts of space between them that have never known human footfall. The map I carried – part of the only useful series of charts available for Antarctica – still featured large areas annotated with comments like 'group of low peaks reported 1965'. I can only assume that no one has been back since to check.

I think it is perhaps Antarctica's lack of human history that forms the essence of its magnetism, the reason why so many are irresistibly drawn to it. In the South, we are presented forcefully with the reality of our frailty and the certainty of our irrelevance to the natural forces working around us. Antarctica shrugs us off without effort. The continent makes me feel vulnerable, both as an individual and as a species. Like views of Earth from space, a view of the Antarctic plateau brings man dramatically into contact with his own limitations. It bludgeons him over the head with the knowledge that nature on our own planet, never mind in the solar system and universe beyond, is far greater, far larger, far older and more limitless than we will ever be. On the plateau we are still no more than precarious visitors. Perhaps that is why this continent more than any other fascinates us, terrifies us, brings us to new understanding and demands deferential respect. To travel through Antarctica is to glimpse existence before man.

Antarctica is elemental and that, I think, forms the core of its addictive attraction.

As I stood looking at my view of a thousand kilometres I wished, not for the first time, that I could magically teleport my Dad from home in England to stand beside me so that we could share this moment. I so dearly wish he could experience for himself – even if only for a moment – the Antarctica I have been allowed to see. I am certain he would be filled with the same deep sense of exhilaration. It feels strange that those closest to me are likely never to encounter the place that has absorbed so much of my life.

I remembered that during my first expedition to the South Pole I had etched the letters '4 Mum + Dad' in the hard packed snow of the eighty-ninth degree with a fat gloved finger and taken a photograph of the crude phrase in the foreground of an empty Antarctic horizon: white crystalline snow, solid indigo-blue sky. I had meant to give them the image in a frame – my gift of a small fragment of place and time in Antarctica dedicated exclusively to them – but it occurred to me now that I had never got around to it. The words I had etched would be long gone but I like to believe that the sentiment they expressed is still there somewhere, locked in the ice.

Like a perfect reflection in calm water that is destroyed by the slightest of disturbances, my sense of an infinite horizon was lost as soon as I moved towards it. It had been a number of days since I had battled through the last of the tortuous ground and giant sastrugi of the eighty-seventh degree. The character of the landscape around me had stealthily transformed day by day. Gone was the brutal flatness of the higher latitudes surrounding the Pole, where the unrelenting horizontal of the terrain had seemed to compress sightlines into stern perpendiculars. Here my surroundings gave the impression of being increasingly fluid. There was more curve, more flex, as if the laws of physics had loosened their grip slightly on the ground around me.

At first it was easy to believe it was nothing but my imagination as often the contours of the landscape were visible only as a change in the hues of the snow; a bright band gleaming proud of the ground before it, or a dusky blueberry bruise hinting at a dell. But eventually I came across gradients and slants that were unmistakable. My sledges at times seemed to glide behind me without effort, as if they had become temporarily weightless – a sure sign that I was skiing downhill. Occasionally when I stopped the sledges would continue moving, sliding to a gentle halt with a nudge at the back of my booted ankles.

Along with the terrain, the texture of the snow under my skis changed and became softer too – transformed into a shiny slick. It reminded me of a sheet of rigid and brittle plastic that becomes pliable as it is warmed, the surface morphing into flowing dimples and becoming shiny with the heat.

It had felt significantly warmer ever since the wind had swung around to be almost consistently at my back. I had stopped wearing a fleece under my windproof jacket and my face mask stayed dry and pliable rather than the solid ice-frozen shell of weeks gone by. The sun is strong in Antarctica despite the cold temperatures and its radiation unfiltered. Its heat can feel dense, concentrated and unremitting. I hoped the better weather was a sign that I was beginning to descend towards the coast and lower altitudes where it would be warmer but I was aware, even then, that this was only a limited reprieve. The longer the good weather lasted, the more I dreaded the inevitable return of the wind and the whiteouts. I regularly scoured the sky for signs of a turn, glaring viciously at any skulking cloud that dared to raise a dirty head above the knife-sharp parapet of a horizon. Several times the weather gathered at the edges of the sky, sliding in stealthy grey daubs along the skyline to my right and left. I'd watch uneasily as the cloud periodically bunched up in intimidating fronts on the horizon. One evening I eyed an advancing weather front fearfully while pitching the Hilleberg, pausing before I ducked through the door to stand and face the oncoming cloud. It seemed unavoidable that while I slept this veil of sun-stealing cloud and vapour would entomb me in the limited visibility I dreaded. I felt a sudden swell of fury and found myself roaring at the sky.

'GO AWAAAY!'

I yelled with such violence that it felt like a blow to the chest. The sound of my own voice, startlingly loud and raw, rang in my ears as I continued to glare at the weather. Under my ferocious gaze the front impassively continued its insidious gathering of grey and gloom, seemingly unperturbed by my outburst. I felt a little silly as I turned to crawl into the tent.

The next morning the front had disappeared without a trace. Perhaps my outburst had had the required effect after all. The sky above me was a perfect dome of blue without so much as a wisp of vestigial cloud. The sun sat alone in the sky, encircled by a perfect halo, the colours of the rainbow percolating from its outer edge. A lively wind as constant as a jet stream blew from the south, raising the drift on the ground like early morning vapour that rises from the waters of a still lake in summertime. The sharpness of the cold air in my nose brought tears to my eyes and a sudden acuity. Everything around me seemed full of light as if brand new. Every edge was definite, every colour true, every sound distinct. Nothing was soiled, or worn or blunted. New tears filled my eyes, this time from pure and concentrated wonder.

I called out my usual greetings to the sun with genuine joy, smiling as I packed away my camp. Waving thanks to the ground beneath my tent for both a restful sleep and a fantastic morning I skied away happily. I travelled that day with my jacket open, wide vents fully unzipped down the sides to reveal my thermals underneath. The zips of my insulated salopettes were undone too, right the way from thigh to ankle, allowing the brisk breeze to cool my thermal wrapped legs, the cuffs of my leggings tucked into knee-length wool socks above my boots. Skiing with long, smooth strides over an icy surface that was cracked like a salt pan, I breathed deeply and smoothly in an easy rhythm. The cough that had disturbed both my skiing during the day and my sleep during the night in weeks past had gone completely and it had been a while since I'd noticed any problems with my kit. My watch, tested and reliable at temperatures down to −40°C, had begun to lose time randomly throughout the coldest days but had now returned to its dependable timekeeping self; and my stove no longer belched noxious fumes as it had done on the highest part of the route for reasons that had defied all my attempts at troubleshooting. Best of all − my lighters worked again. It couldn't be more different from my memories of the 'wrong side' of Antarctica.

Despite my easy progress the countdown to the last day of the season was never far from my mind and in an effort to make the most of the advantageous conditions while they lasted I put pressure on myself to be as efficient as possible. I was careful to keep my breaks brief and I continued as late into the day as I dared. I carried out my regular chores in the tent as quickly as possible, constantly making small time-saving adjustments to my routines in order to get to sleep just a few minutes earlier. Each night I was asleep as early as I could manage. When I wasn't asleep, I wanted to be on my skis covering as many of the remaining miles as I could.

The combination of good weather, glassy surfaces and occasional downhill sections began to make a difference to my daily mileages so that I was regularly covering fifteen, then eighteen, nautical miles in a day.

On 2 January, my thirty-ninth day, I sat cross-legged in the tent staring open-mouthed at the figures on the GPS unit in my hand. I had covered exactly twenty nautical miles. In my pre-expedition planning it would have seemed ridiculously audacious to propose this kind of mileage as a daily target. On my way across the 'wrong side' of Antarctica to the South Pole my best day had seen me cover sixteen nautical miles and that was on a near-ice surface with a practically empty sledge. I had not expected to do any better than that on the second leg of my journey and yet, in the days that followed I consistently skied more than twenty nautical miles – again and again.

I marvelled at the distances I recorded but worried what this spurt of mileage might be taking out of me. Polar travel had always struck me as a war of attrition. Each day of exposure to the extremes of Antarctica made me a little weaker – the constant physical exertion having the same negative effects as overtraining. Every evening I felt weighed down by physical tiredness, crawling around my tent on hands and knees as I pitched it because standing was too much effort. Sleep came like a computer monitor blinking to lifeless black and waking felt like a fight against gravity to rise to the surface of a peat bog. One morning I lay in my sleeping bag, eyes closed, trying to isolate all the different aches and pains. Every single component of my body from my toenails to the top of my head seemed to be complaining loudly and uncomfortably. Even my thoughts hurt. It seemed impossible that this mass of protesting muscle and bone would be able to take another step but every day, with the help of generous doses of ibuprofen and paracetamol and a belief in the mechanical endurance of my body's engineering, clipping into the skis seemed to bind everything together. I'd move forward gently at first, allowing my muscles to remember the too-familiar movements, feeling uncoordinated, jerky and unsteady. But I'd notice with a slight sense of pride that astonishingly quickly the stiffness would evaporate and each halting movement flowed more smoothly into the next until my body fell, without coercion, into the usual rhythm. While skiing I didn't feel as if I was pushing myself beyond reason and knowing the mileage I was logging seemed to lift me. It made me feel invincible.

As a treat to celebrate my good mood and better progress, I allowed myself to listen to the audio material I'd been saving on my MP3 player. Until now I'd listened only to music. I'd learnt from previous expeditions that deciding what music to take on a journey is actually quite difficult to get right. Variety is the key because no matter how much you love a particular genre, album or band, over the course of six weeks or more it begins to get tedious. (Preparing for this expedition I had made the mistake of asking friends for contributions from their music collections to bolster the variety in my own and began to notice a theme in the tracks I received in response; Cypress Hill – 'Insane in the Brain'; James Blunt – 'Out of My Mind'; Garbage – 'Stupid Girl'; Green Day – 'Basket Case'; Eminem – 'Just Lose It'; The Eurythmics – 'Don't Ask Me

Why'.) Eventually, I had decided to add variety by adding spoken word recordings. My Dad gave me a complete set of BBC Radio 4's *Sceptred Isle* series – over 300 hours of British history from the ancient Britons to Queen Victoria. This might not be everyone's ideal but I love history, so I loaded every single episode onto my MP3 player.

Unfortunately, what I didn't realise was that my particular player logged each individual programme as a separate track and replayed the tracks not in the order they had been downloaded but in alphabetical order according to the title of the episode. What this meant was that I had 300 hours of British history played at me in a totally random order over which I had no control. As I skied through a blissfully serene Antarctica, the digital voice in my ears darted from medieval England to the Age of Enlightenment, from the Spanish Armada to the American War of Independence. This might have been fine was it not for the fact that the British monarchy hasn't been very imaginative through the ages when it comes to naming their first born. There are a lot of Edwards, a lot of Georges, and a lot of Henrys. I very quickly lost track of precisely which King was riding into battle and it appeared that the very same Henry was rampaging through British History lopping the heads off of everything from the Vikings to the Victorians.

I had the same problem with audio books. Each chapter was logged as a separate track and the tracks were played in alphabetical order according to title. Listening to an Agatha Christie murder mystery, I heard the murderer revealed before anyone had actually been murdered.

In frustration I returned to listening to music. As I skied along contentedly listening to an eclectic selection of tracks I turned my head to gaze with narrowed eyes on the sun away to my left. It was a shimmering ornament of intense white light tinged with the pale gold of Champagne, a froth of highly charged atoms expanding through space.

'Champagne Supernova...' sang the lyrics of the song playing in my ears.

The name was perfect.

'You are my Champagne Supernova,' I said aloud to the sun.

'Don't call me that,' it snapped back, the voice clear and distinct in my head.

The sun was too majestic to be given nicknames.

'Nicknames suggest familiarity,' it emphasised haughtily.

I tried to explain that the nickname was a mark of affection, of gratitude, that the name implied beauty and awe – but the sun was not to be persuaded. Regardless, I knew that, from now on, I would always think of the sun as my magnificent Champagne Supernova.

'I can hear your thoughts,' blazed the voice of the sun in my head, unamused.

'But it's such a pity,' I protested. 'It's a great name.'

I blinked upward at the intense light before being struck with the sudden realisation that I was talking to the sun. What was worse, it was talking back. I could distinctly hear its words in my head. Was I going mad?

I didn't feel insane – but then I assume nobody does. How could I know for sure? I recalled the warning of my friend at the Royal Geographical Society that those who set out alone came back 'changed', and my worries that the solitude in Antarctica might leave me a little odd. The worst outcome I could envision was that, while others were aware I had become slightly strange, I would be oblivious to my own eccentricity.

'As long as you are aware, on some level, that the hallucinations aren't real, you'll be fine,' Dr Pack had reassured me before I'd left the UK. 'It's only when you are unable to tell what is reality that it becomes a clinical problem.'

I considered his words. Did I know that the sun wasn't actually speaking to me?

'Careful. I can hear what you are thinking,' warned the sun.

The threat was clear. If I caused affront by pondering the reality of my spectral companion, I would have only myself to blame when the sun consequently disappeared into bad weather and refused to come back. The thought of days without the sun to give contrast, without a guiding light to navigate by, filled me with disproportionate dread. I would do anything to insure against a return to those dreadful days of dimensionless gloom. I apologised earnestly to the sun and tried to erase all thoughts of the psychology of my developing friendship.

'Don't worry,' I placated. 'Of course I know you are real and I'm very grateful for such very real company.'

I turned my face towards the incandescent light and felt its warmth. Irrespective of the reality of the voice in my head, I couldn't doubt that the sun was at least a real physical presence, one that warmed not just my skin but my spirit. My whole body rejoiced in the relief of a sun-filled day. Nothing strange in that, but here it made the difference between contented endurance and a desperate struggle. As if to signify my forgiveness, a prismatic halo circled the sun. The halo branched into a mirror image of itself at each point of the compass, like four multi-coloured smiles. And at each point of contact a flare of rainbow light marked the spot. My heart lifted to meet the spectacle but then soared as I noticed the optics had widened even further, spreading a pale band of light around the sky directly above my head, so that I had to spin 360 degrees in order to see it all. The sun sat in the middle of the arrangement like the crowning jewel of a celestial diadem. On the horizon directly beneath it was a semi-circle of vermillion shine rising from the snow surface, as if the light that hit the ground was throwing up a geometrically perfect plume of dust. I'd seen this blaze before, my guardian angel on the way to the Pole. The sprite was back, and I took it as a good omen.

I had other reasons to feel positive. I was approaching the eighty-sixth line of latitude and I knew that as soon as I crossed into the eighty-fifth degree I would be within sixty nautical miles of Thiels Corner, the place where I expected to collect my second and last resupply and the goal that had become the focus of all my mental energy since leaving the Pole. The target that had seemed so impossibly distant now felt impossibly close – close enough that I almost dared to believe I would reach it. Almost. My superstitious fear of jinxing the outcome prevented me from allowing myself to believe anything until it had happened. I was still on high-alert, my hope and anticipation tightly restricted, my concentration spent on trying to foresee what could go wrong and how I could reduce the likelihood of any potential disaster occurring. Sixty nautical miles was still a long way.

My only distraction was the thought that within the eighty-fifth degree I might stand a chance of spotting the Thiel Mountains away to the west. The idea of seeing some geography filled me with improbable levels of excitement. It wasn't just having something to look at that appealed to me, it would also be proof of my progress. Every night I continued to mark each camp faithfully on my map (a series of crosses which now traced a wonky, twitching line across the page) but it occurred to me, somewhat irrationally, that I had very little real evidence that I had moved at all. Sighting the mountains would change that. My gaze began to flick repeatedly to the westward horizon even though it was hopeless to expect to see anything from this distance. And so it was that I was looking to my left when I sensed rather than saw a dark shadow slip silently across the snow away to my right. A chill not caused by the temperature crept up my spine and made the hair at the back of my neck stand on end with such intensity that it hurt. I snapped my head around to where the shadow had fallen, but it was gone.

Without a pause I continued skiing, trying to make sense of what I had experienced, feeling the alarm behind my eyes. Then I noticed a ripple of darkness passing over the sleeves of my jacket. The shadow was no longer on the snow but sliding over me. I looked straight up but saw nothing above me other than blue sky. Seconds later a violent scream of colour exploded into my vision. Neon pink and lime-green. Not the crystalline colours created by the sun but the bold opaque colours of man-made fibres. It was a parasail. I stopped in my tracks to look behind me and what I saw sent my heart thudding into my throat in shock and surprise. Not a dozen feet behind me stood a team of Norwegian kiters.

I knew the group. I had met them at Union Glacier and again at the South Pole. They were using the winds flowing out from the centre of the plateau to drive them home to the coast. Able to travel a hundred kilometres or more a day quite easily in the right winds, I had assumed they would be a long way ahead of me if not already back at Union Glacier by now. However, it turned out that the calm weather I had enjoyed had not been so welcomed by the kiters. Without wind they could go nowhere.

Twitching on their skis, they were pulled impatiently by the kites bobbing in a holding pattern overhead as we swapped news. They laughed about their bad luck with the weather and I marvelled at how they had been able to cross the rough ground in the eighty-seventh degree with kites. I couldn't imagine how they had been able to find a route through the immense rubble while travelling at speed without smashing their sledges (and themselves) to bits in the process. I explained that with music in my ears I hadn't heard them approaching and they told me that I had appeared as a dark spot on the horizon a few miles back and that they had diverted off their route to investigate.

We didn't speak for long. Unlike my last surreal meeting in the wilderness, this time I was eager to be gone. The banter and the laughter between the group felt, to me, to be too sudden and too harsh, like the shock of a loud radio turned on accidentally. I skied away as the team began to pull their kites out of the sky so that they could stop for a break, but within half an hour they had already overtaken me. I saw them pass me by several kilometres away to the west, a long line of toy-soldier-sized figures pulled by red kites that looked stunningly bold against the delicate blushes of Antarctica. I watched the arc and dive of the kites in the distance as I skied, admiring the grace of the movement – and the speed. Within minutes the figures of the team were indistinguishable from the texture of the landscape and my head began to whirr with mental arithmetic as I tried to calculate what kind of distance they would cover that day. I'm sure kiting long distances has its own frustrations and drawbacks but as I watched the agile sails swoop and spiral toward the horizon it appeared to be the most magnificent and elegant form of motion ever devised and I scorned myself bitterly for deciding against using them.

In no time at all the kites had disappeared beyond my view but occasionally they would briefly reappear as barely perceptible smudges of angular colour in the far distance, floating just above the skyline.

The sense of deflation I felt when the kites vanished for good lingered into the next morning. Despite my initial wariness, the kiters had brought colour, noise and vitality; a sudden and brilliant display of life that left me feeling its absence. All day I found myself automatically scanning the horizon as I had done the day before, scrutinising each shape or shadow – but this time I realised I was as eager for any last sight of the kites as I was for mountains. Several times I thought I could detect a condensed blob of colour, miniscule in the distance, only for it to vanish, leaving me doubting that it had ever been there at all. Similarly the clouds that rose and fell in swells on the horizon were teasingly mountainlike, mimicking summits touched by sunlight or dark weather-shrouded rock, before evaporating.

Then, quite without warning, there they were. A litter of dark purple lumps popped out of the horizon; unmistakably mountains. I stopped dead in stunned wonder, stumbling on my skis as I swung my head in a double-take. Thiel Mountains – the first geography I had seen since leaving the Transantarctic Mountains more than a month ago. A slow grin spread through my face, stretching the cold, reluctant skin of my cheeks.

All day the mountains sprang in and out of view, fragments and jags of dark rock against the shimmering landscape. Gradually they began to coalesce and join together into a single chain of peak and plateau, growing in size until they loomed large on the horizon in perfect view. I couldn't help but ski with my head permanently turned to the left, gawking at the developing scenery. I knew these were the Thiel Mountains but they didn't match in size or form the detailed memory I had of them from three years before when I had passed them with the team, or the snapshot I could remember so clearly from the air. If not for map and GPS I would never have recognised them.

I felt a swelling of overwhelming happiness building in my chest. It was a contented, uncomplicated happiness – that particular kind of straightforward pleasure that comes with a blissful stretch, or sinking deliciously into a freshly made bed – and it was a glee that couldn't be contained.

'I'm happy,' I called aloud to the sky. 'I'm so very, very happy!'

I skied for the rest of the day unable to stop smiling and camped with my tent deliberately positioned to allow a view of the mountains from my usual perch inside the vestibule, close to the stove. In the calm weather and with the extra heat from the stove temporarily filling the small space within the Hilleberg I was able to leave the doorway hanging open as I melted snow and chewed on my food, savouring the view as much as the meal. I registered only the pleasure of feeling the warmth of the sun through the tent fabric, the contentment of feet tucked into plump booties of warm down and the enjoyment of mouthfuls of hot, tasty food slowly filling my hunger. Life was uncomplicated and it felt effortlessly fulfilling. The alone-ness that evening wasn't full of terror, it was instead a seductive form of peace.

On Saturday 7 January, the forty-fourth day of my expedition, I woke to silence and the blinding brightness of the sun shining through the side of the tent with all the vibrancy of an illuminated stained glass window. I knew from my GPS that I was a little over thirteen nautical miles from my resupply at Thiels Corner and I was determined not to stop that day until I found it. Over the previous two days I had skied more than forty-six nautical miles, so I had reason to feel confident but, as ever, I was careful to strap down tightly any rising optimism for fear of a jinx. As I prepared breakfast quietly in the stillness I unzipped the door of the tent so that I could look at the mountains on the horizon. Sunlight exploded from the polished snow surfaces of the high plateaus, linking the mafic black of individual peaks. I was unwilling to sully such a perfect morning with the horror of porridge. Even after forty-four days I hadn't managed to override the aversion I'd developed on my first day. It still made me gag and required attentive will-power to force digestion of what I could now only see as unappetising gloop. I pulled an evening meal from my sledge and ate pasta for breakfast instead. I took my time, lingering over my coffee and treating myself to extra chocolate from that evening's rations. Sunlight was everywhere, beating down on the tent and radiating through the fabric as if the sun was deliberately trying to attract my attention.

'Good Morning!' I called from inside the Hilleberg. 'Thanks for such an awesome day. It is really appreciated.'

I sensed that the sun was in a charming mood and was relieved. Recently my companion had become increasingly petulant, demanding endless flattery and compliment for its brilliance in return for its continued presence. It was getting a little trying.

I set off feeling as if I could float. Today, rather than me pulling myself over the snow, it seemed as if the landscape was being rolled around on a conveyor beneath me. I was reduced to playing the role of an actor pretending to ski in front of a bluescreen. It felt almost effortless. After an hour or so I gazed down at my feet in contemplation, watching them push forward one after the other in turn. I noticed that with each push I seemed to glide further than expected and it slowly dawned on me that I wasn't simply being carried forward by euphoria, but by gravity. I was skiing down a gentle incline with enough gradient that I was able to glide almost without effort, using momentum alone. The motion became more pronounced until I could push myself forward using only my ski poles. I whooped aloud at the discovery, delighted at being able to use a different technique and at the modest sensation of speed.

Looking ahead I noticed the horizon shorten, as if I was approaching an edge. I stopped to try and understand what I was looking at and noticed that my sledge slid to a leisurely halt, not behind me as usual, but to one side, threatening to overtake me. The forward view was soft and blended with the texture of a dream and at first my brain struggled to make sense of the information received from my eyes. Flat splodges of cloud cast confusing shadows which pockmarked the ground and obliterated any perspective. To my left the mountains stood sentinel-like in streaks of purple and gold. Catching sight of them gave sudden scale to the scene and my mind reeled at the realisation of how far I could see. Finally, I could appreciate the magnitude of the slope below me. I approached the lip cautiously, eager to feel the glide of the gradient and yet filled with unease, like a nervous rider on the summit of a roller coaster. I soon felt the pull of gravity, my skis sliding onwards beneath me as if by themselves, their metal edges rasping roughly on the icy surface. I found that I could keep my skis parallel to each other, not moving my feet at all, and simply propel myself forward with my poles. Then, as I gathered speed, I stopped paddling with my poles and used them for balance instead, messily jabbing the ground to keep myself upright. It had been a long time since I had needed to keep my balance and it didn't feel instinctive. I felt a violent tug to the right and realised that my sledges, as eager as an excited puppy, had broken ranks from behind me and now raced alongside, threatening to overtake. I brought myself to a safe halt – just to prove that I could – before taking off again, whooping aloud at the thrill of it. I allowed myself to go as fast as I dared. I had no means (nor sufficient skill) to steer on free-heeled skis over such hard ground at speed, so I simply clattered clumsily over ripples of stone-hard sastrugi, concentrating instead on balance. Eventually the rush of exhilaration turned into a fizz of fear. It was clear that a fall could be potentially disastrous. Yet I was enjoying myself too much to stop and delighted by the thought of the effortless miles I was covering so rapidly. I flew down the hill, sledges bumping and bucking at my side, squealing and grinning like a child on a toboggan. When the gradient eventually flattened out and I drew gently to a halt, still giggling to myself, I decided to take an early break to calm the nerves that remained tense from all the excitement. Pushing a fistful of snacks into my mouth and pulling out my water bottle, I looked up at the slope above me. It reared into the sky like a monster and I felt grateful that I wasn't travelling in the opposite direction.

Invigorated as I was by the rapid descent, the thought of Thiels Corner drew me on. I was regularly skiing around three and a half nautical miles in the ninety minutes between each break, so by my fourth leg I knew I was close. I pulled out my GPS from under layers of clothing and knowingly sacrificed some battery power in order to leave the unit switched on in my pocket and regularly check that I was heading in precisely the right direction. The ground ahead was crowded with sastrugi rising in rounded thigh-high moguls creating shadows on the snow. My eyes darted from one patch of shade to another trying to detect anything more distinct from the rest. My sight returned nervously to one particular spot in the far distance.

I was looking at an object and not a shadow.

The anticipation was so acute that I must have stopped breathing because I found myself short on air, my eyes never moving from the dark object up ahead. When I noticed two smaller flickering dark spots above the object, I was sure. This had to be a depot marked by two crossed flags on long canes.

It could only be my resupply.

This was Thiels Corner.

Relief and joy flooded through me, spilling over as tears and I wept out loud as I skied. I laughed and sobbed, feeling a peculiar mix of elation and anguish, my vision distorted by crying. I couldn't help but think of all those dark days on the Leverett so long ago where any hope of reaching this point had seemed so futile; all those desperate mornings battling with my mind, all those evenings since leaving the Pole faithfully marking my progress on an empty map, endlessly calculating distances and days. Ill-defined snapshots of sensations or places I had experienced in the previous weeks flicked in and out of my mind. The snapshots were often no more than an echo of a moment of fear, the remembrance of an instant of wonder, a recollection of light falling through an abating blizzard, or the detail of a wayward snowflake settled on my jacket sleeve – but together they coalesced into a tapestry of experiences that I could barely believe were safely in my past. Whatever happened now, these memories were forever a part of my life experiences and would shape me as all experiences do, becoming an inextricable part of who I will be. There was anguish recalling all the difficult emotions of the past weeks and reliving them slightly in the process – but it was matched by the elation of knowing that I had faced all those emotional trials and reached this point in spite of them. As I skied those last metres to the depot I allowed myself to dwell on the journey so far and it left me with a feeling of pride.

At the depot I found a cluster of fuel drums lashed together in the snow and, a few paces away, a knotted black bin liner shored up with dunes of drift on the ground. Two willowy canes crossed over the bag like guardians, each cane topped with a small black pennant twitching in the constant breeze – the flickering dark spots I had seen from a distance. I pitched my tent close by without touching the depot.

It was a sun-filled day so I was able to empty the remaining contents of my sledges onto the snow to take stock of what I had. Having reached the resupply at least five days quicker than expected, I found I had much more stove fuel than I would need. I didn't want to carry the extra weight so my only option was to use it – and I knew immediately what I wanted more than anything else, barring company. With the tent door wide open I melted pan after pan of snow on the stove until I had filled every container I possessed with hot water. For the first time since leaving Union Glacier I took off all my clothes then, placing a foam sleeping mat on the snow outside the tent door, I stepped, naked, into the polar chill. I felt the cold on my skin but with nothing more than a breeze stirring the air it felt only refreshing, like stepping out of a stuffy room into the open.

Having arranged the water-filled containers within easy reach I grabbed the first, closed my eyes and lifted my face to the sky as I poured deliciously warm water slowly and deliberately over my head. The sensation was ecstatic. There is something deeply primeval about pouring hot water over our heads; it is as comforting and uplifting as being wrapped in a hug. The water was cold by the time it reached my ankles but it didn't matter. I poured each container in turn over my head and shoulders until the water pooled around my feet. I eked out the last drenching for as long as possible, relishing every last drop, but when it was over I was quick to hop back into the shelter of the tent where I had left myself a fresh clean sock with which to dry off. I zipped up the doors of the Hilleberg and pulled the roaring stove inside the small sleeping compartment so that it was soon as hot as a dry sauna.

Only then did I truly look at myself and what I saw was shocking. It wasn't so much that I had lost weight, it was the fact that my entire body shape had changed. I didn't recognise my own limbs. My knees were bony protruding lumps above razor-sharp shins that were wrapped near the ankle by pouches of firm muscle. My thighs were the size my calves used to be and my bum had all but disappeared. As I strained to look behind me I could see that each buttock caved in at my hip rather than the usually over-generous curve outward. But it was perhaps my arms that were most unfamiliar; they seemed to be lumpy in all the wrong places. The skin was stretched over new muscle as tightly as an overstuffed suitcase. I took out my tiny palm-sized mirror that I used for checking my face for signs of cold injury and tried to take in my new figure. I caught a glimpse of my back, as unattractively lumpy with muscle as my arms, and I noticed that my head appeared to be ludicrously large in relation to my limbs, as if it might fall off my neck when shaking my head. As the shock of the change wore off, I strained to look behind me again and felt a smile cross my face. I couldn't pretend to be too upset that I now had the buttocks of an athlete.

The heat from the stove dried me off quickly and I covered my skin in a generous layer of suncream to moisturise it. Gingerly I took a closer look in the mirror at a sore patch that had developed on my behind. I knew what it was because I'd had it before: chilblains. It is a cold injury caused by repeated exposure to extreme cold followed by rapid warming that is often called 'Arctic Thigh', despite the fact that it can occur anywhere on the legs or hind quarters. When the skin is cold, chilblains are completely painless but as soon as the skin starts to thaw out and warm up each chilblain becomes maddeningly itchy. It is important (although nearly impossible) not to itch the damaged skin but even so, over time each chilblain gets larger until it becomes a nasty open sore. At this point it is excruciating when knocked and in my case, painful to sit on. My chilblain was already the size of a rosette, the centre a dark, ugly purple, the skin having died away around it in concentric circles of angry red, then inflamed pink. What was worse, I noticed several other smaller chilblains on my buttocks and thighs that were likely to deteriorate quickly. I slathered the area in antiseptic cream and was careful to lie on my side in the tent so as not to antagonise the sores any further – though the only thing that would make the sore heal completely would be going home.

Rescuing the lonely bin liner from the depot I emptied the contents into the tent for sorting. I knew what was inside because I had packed the bag myself almost two months before – twenty ration bags each containing breakfast, snacks, dinner and supplements for a single day – but as I reached the bottom of the bag I found a parcel that I hadn't packed. Inside were four chunky home-baked cookies. The smell of oats and cranberries brought drool into my mouth even as I carefully unwrapped the tin foil around them. I devoured one instantly, fussily ensuring every crumb was eaten, before stashing the rest for later. As I replaced the cookies in their packaging I noticed a white notepaper folded into quarters underneath them. It was from a member of staff at Union Glacier.

'You are almost done!' it cheered. 'Know that there are so many people here and abroad cheering you on and thinking about you every day...'

I couldn't read the rest because my eyes had clogged with tears. The thought that I was remembered, that someone had gone to all the effort and energy to leave me encouragement when they knew I would need it most was touching and uplifting. The impact of such thoughtfulness by a near stranger when I had been without proper human contact for so long was huge. The note took on immense significance and gave me renewed purpose. It made me feel less isolated in the same way that sending one-way SMS messages from my satphone into the ether every day made me feel less alone.

I was now just 300 nautical miles from Hercules Inlet on the coast of Antarctica where I had planned to finish my journey. Barely a week earlier the prospect of completing my traverse before the end of the season had seemed impossibly remote. The highest expectation I had allowed myself was to reach my second resupply before the plane from Union Glacier was sent to fetch me. And yet, as I lay in my tent at Thiels Corner waiting for sleep, I grappled with disbelief at the fact that not only was the once-distant goal achieved, but it had also been achieved significantly ahead of schedule. I had reached my second resupply considerably before the looming deadline and it changed everything. For the first time since leaving the Leverett, it seemed possible that I could make it to the coast.

I had, at best, twenty days until Steve would want me back at Union Glacier. The last 300 nautical miles of my journey had gone quickly but I'd had good weather and favourable terrain. What lay ahead was flat and prone to deep snow, not to mention week-long storms that pinned teams in their tents and my sledges, renewed with the resupply, were back to full weight. It was impossible to predict whether twenty days would be enough – but there was enough opportunity to leave me optimistic. I could feel an unhealthy desperation building. In the past I had placated myself with covenants to get as far as I could but now, there was no denying that to be this close and not make the coast would be worse, far worse, than having given up at the Pole. Previously, I had not allowed myself to believe there was any hope and that had suppressed any sense of need. Now that I had a chance, I felt taut with the pressure of it. For the first time, I became aware of the truth – that anything less than the coast would be a crushing disappointment.

CHAPTER EIGHT

SKIING IN THE DARK

@felicity_aston A steely day in Antarctica with grey skies, dark weather and flat light. Still managed 22.5nm but was relieved to get back in the tent.

@felicity_aston With less than 70nm to go I was hoping to get my 1st glimpse of the mountains today. Scanned the horizons all day – nothing.

@felicity_aston Stomping through fresh snow has aggravated my grumbling knees. I keep pleading with them to hold it together for just one more week...

Privacy was rare during my life at Rothera Research Station. It was an odd paradox to be so isolated from the world and yet living so closely with others. During the seven-month winters with a crew of just twenty I found that it was important to be comfortable in my own company as well as highly sociable in order to handle such a small and tight community. Twice a year each member of the wintering team was allowed a 'holiday'. We weren't able to leave the continent but we could take snowmobiles and a companion for a week-long camping trip into the local area around the base. It doesn't sound like much, but this short sojourn into the Antarctic night was one of very few opportunities for respite from the claustrophobia of the base and everyone looked forward to it.

The tents were heavy double-lined pyramids of orange Ventile that were luxuriously spacious inside. When a Tilley lamp was lit within the tent, the light glowed through the fabric so that, from outside, it looked like a bonfire.

During my final winter trip at Rothera a blizzard had raged in the darkness of polar night outside the tent for nearly three days without easing once. Outside, it was an apocalyptic fury of wind and snow but inside, my holiday companion and I were so well ensconced that the noise of the storm was muted to nothing more than a dim rumble that was almost soothing – a natural lullaby of moving air. We'd spent the time sleeping, reading and eating meals imaginatively and elaborately created from the basic dried supplies we had with us, helpless in the ferocity of an Antarctic winter storm to do anything but wait. There was only one reason to leave the warmth and comfort of the tent.

Having put it off for hours, I wearily pulled on layers and a headtorch before pushing myself through the narrow tubular entrance of the tent into another world. In the dark I pushed forward against the wind, away from the tent towards where our snowmobiles would now be completely buried in drift and snowfall. Behind me the tent glowed brightly through the blowing snow like an orange beacon. I kept a careful eye on it as I stepped as far as I dared into the dark. I didn't want to get lost in the low visibility. The storm didn't feel so violent now that I was exposed to it. In fact, it felt good to be outside and alone.

Perhaps it was the enjoyment of a snatched moment of solitude that lured me into taking too long. I suddenly realised that my hands and feet were far too cold. Dangerously cold. Rather than a friendly place of comfortable seclusion, the storm suddenly seemed like a treacherous trap. I ploughed into the blizzard toward the brightness of the tent but it seemed a long way off. I didn't remember walking so far. The beam from my headtorch stopped a few feet ahead of me, blotted out by the snow in the air and obscuring my fix on the tent, so I turned it off. Unable to pick out my tracks on the ground I plunged my booted but frozen feet into fresh shin-deep snow, stumbling as I broke through the surface crust, and balanced myself with my gloved hands leaving them encrusted with wet ice.

The tent didn't seem to be getting any closer. I fell on the ground but didn't get up. Instead I sat in the cold with my arms crossed so that each hand was buried under an arm for some warmth and looked at the tent shining brightly in the near distance. The snow rushed past my face in long streaks and the drift began to create white dunes around me. The tent was too far. I couldn't reach it. Any effort to move seemed pointless and I knew without trying that any shouts for help would be carried away on the wind. There was nothing to be done, I told myself, except sit and let the snow take me. I was completely aware of the consequences but accepted them with sad resignation. I could feel the cold creeping in but it felt oddly relaxing, like sinking into the softest of sofas.

Too absorbed in a contented apathy to be aware of time, I don't know how long I sat in the snow, neither do I know what it was that shook me from my cold-enduced trance but I remember a sudden awakening.

What was I doing?

Scrambling to my feet, I threw myself through the wind towards the tent, pushing onwards until, gasping for breath, I fell against the mound of trampled snow heaped against the entrance. With a last fearful glance out into the dark, I forced my head and shoulders awkwardly through the circular doorway and into the warmth.

'You OK?' asked my companion casually as I sat by the entrance brushing snow from my clothing and breathing heavily.

I said nothing but I felt shaken to my core. As I warmed my feet, hands and face with urgency, forcing the blood back into my fingers, my mind went over what had just happened in silent disbelief. Just a few moments earlier I had been willing to sit in the snow and fall asleep forever. I was shocked at the betrayal by my own mind.

I had heard stories of people becoming mentally disorientated by hypothermia but it seemed unlikely that my body temperature had fallen low enough to be hypothermic. I couldn't find an easy explanation and it troubled me. It was frightening to believe that the mind I had considered to be unquestionably dependable, the brain I trusted, could be so easily confused into making a potential lethal decision. What control do we have if we cannot rely on our own mind?

The experience had haunted me ever since. I saw it as a demonstration of just how fragile our foundations of thought can be. The brain is, after all, nothing more than chemicals and biology. Now, as I crept northward across the eighty-fourth line of latitude on my crossing of the continent I was aware, on some level, that my psychological patterns and processes had subtly changed. At the outset, in the face of Antarctica's brutal monotony, it had been vitally important for me to keep my mind occupied, to develop my daydreams into time-consuming mental peregrinations – elongated musings that would absorb my concentration and eat up the hours as my pace ate up the miles. Hitting on a good avenue of thought felt as satisfying to me as striking a seam of gold in a rockface. I would zealously pursue the thread right to its very end until the seam was scoured of every possible ounce of material. But now, after more than six weeks on the ice by myself, I could ski for hours without being aware of a single notion passing through my head. Sometimes whole days would pass without me thinking much at all. The endless repetitive rhythm of movement had slowly leached all substance from my brain until it felt like I was existing without conscious thought; being without thinking. But instead of the emptiness in my head driving me to insanity with boredom as before, now I was content with the emptiness. Thinking demanded energy and I didn't have any energy to spare. I was incapable of anything except robotically following routine. When it came to my daily calls to Union Glacier to report my position I found the switch between self-contained silence and light-hearted exchange with the voices on the other end increasingly difficult. Communication with Union Glacier had never been chatty, it had a serious purpose and was treated as such, but I found myself cutting out all pleasantries entirely so that the interaction was no more than a brief transfer of information. I couldn't muster the vigour for anything but the basics. Preserving what energy I had left felt like re-entering that state of mental hibernation that I had cultivated when leaving the UK. I even stopped talking to myself. This most instinctive of coping mechanisms that had been so immediate when I was first left alone by the plane on the Ross Ice Shelf had now petered out almost completely. These days the only dialogue was that taking place in my head with the sun. Usually the first words I spoke aloud during the day were those few lines to Union Glacier shortly after crawling back into my tent at the end of a day skiing. Once or twice I started to speak into the satellite phone only to find that I had lost my voice and it would take me a second to recover, my speech sounding halting and husky as if I'd already forgotten how to use it.

Around me Antarctica had once more faded into the soft greys and melancholy tones of overcast weather. It was heartbreakingly desolate and yet as surreal and otherworldly as a dream. Drifting snow broiled along the ground and in the air making everything appear fuzzy around the edges. It seemed like the whole of Antarctica was on the move and I often felt as if I was skiing over cloud tops with the softness of pillows and silk. Only the very tips of the curled ends of my skis protruded above the constantly shifting drift, so that all I could see was two black mice scurrying ahead of me at a regular distance, racing each other, each one winning and losing in turn. I could feel the increasing volume of fine loess deposited beneath the drift and cushioning my skis in a way that felt almost sumptuous despite the extra effort of carving through it. The snow in the air wasn't the hard icy pellets or the frozen vapour of higher latitudes but thick, fat flakes of Christmas snow, falling so thickly that they eventually blotted out the horizon. Antarctica became a speckled world the colours of ash and smoke.

In the dissolving landscape I restricted my focus to my immediate surroundings so that my route took on a solid form in my mind as an unbroken line leading me across the ice. I concentrated on this imagined pathway as if it was the only thing fixing me firmly on the ground. It seemed that if I let my brain expand to take in the true vastness of the space around me, to accurately appreciate the scale of my isolation, I was sure that it would expand beyond my control and that I would never be able to get it all back into my head. I worried that by opening my mind to the immensity of Antarctica I would be in danger of losing myself completely. It was a psychological vulnerability as real as any physical hazard but wasn't something I had ever experienced before. The sensation resembled walking a knife-edge ridge in the mountains with a sheer drop on either side. The void can be sensed without looking and even though the temptation might be to glance into the view below, instinct quickly returns your focus to the ridge ahead. For if you stare for too long, or too deeply into that abyss, it might pull you off balance and you will fall. I often made a point of stopping to look at and take in my surroundings, but it was always with caution. I never let my mind open up to the space completely and I was always quick to return my focus to the unseen but clearly perceived route ahead.

I could see myself from above as a tiny green dot inching across the gentle contours of the landscape, isolated and vulnerable in a grey wilderness with charcoal clouds and titanium snow, so far from anywhere and anyone. The vision was achingly depressing, and yet, at the same time there was wonder in it. I stopped and lifted my face skywards, pulling aside my mask so that I felt the gentle brush of each feathery

Christmas-flake on my skin and when I looked up I noticed that the sky was blue overhead even though the snow fell thickly from it. The moment felt as miraculous as it was intimidating. I tried to force my sluggish brain to remember every detail as I skied away because I was sure it was a memory I wanted to keep; an illustration of the dual nature of this most contrary of continents.

The Christmas snow was a moment of calm in what was becoming a tightly anxious day. I was approaching a known area of crevasses unnervingly marked on my map and in my GPS with a stylised symbol of a skull and crossbones. The information had been passed on by Steve at ALE who had collected reported sightings from previous expeditions. Each expedition had come across only one or two crevasses but together the sightings formed a tight cluster. I couldn't bank on the accuracy of the plots on my GPS and neither was there any way of knowing how extensive the crevassed area might be. With this in mind I had been deliberately veering my course eastwards over the previous few days as a precaution to avoid the area completely. I didn't want to risk coming across any outlying crevasses. Even so, the proximity of the skull and crossbones made me uneasy. In the overcast weather and the heavy spindrift it was hard to spot any strange formations on the surface even though I scrutinised the ground minutely as I skied, avoiding anything that looked suspiciously geometrical or linear.

Then I stopped in surprise.

Quite suddenly, no more than a few inches from my right ski, I noticed clear vehicle tracks. I looked again, more carefully. Patterns of wind erosion in the snow had the habit of taking on familiar forms and in the past weeks I had repeatedly thought I saw the tracks of vehicles or of other skiers only to find myself mistaken on a second look. This time there was no mistake. The tracks were eroded at the edges and flattened by the wind but there was the clear crosshatching of tyre treads that couldn't be natural. They were clear enough for me to be able to follow them with my gaze from where I stood. They extended behind me for four or five metres and ahead of me the same. I skied on alongside them, easily picking out the hard unnatural edge of the tracks as I moved. At first I followed them absent-mindedly out of casual curiosity but as they continued to lead eastwards on more or less my exact heading I found myself becoming increasingly dependent. The association of the tracks with the presence of others made me reluctant to leave them, as if I felt closer to civilisation by being nearby. I was sure that whatever vehicle had made these tracks was long gone but knowing that people had passed this exact spot in the past offered the illusion of protection from the dangers of the snowpack.

In fact there were no such guarantees. The tracks could be old and the ice underneath them might have shifted since they were made. The condition of the snow might have changed too. A snowbridge over a crevasse that is solid enough to take the weight of a vehicle at the beginning of the season might disintegrate under its own weight after an entire summer of sunshine and wind erosion. The tracks, for the moment, headed in the same direction as the needle on my compass but there was no telling where they would go and whether they would travel there in a straight line. Following a winding track would add unnecessary miles to my route – extra time I could ill afford. Nevertheless, in my emotional need I ignored all this common sense. In that moment the tracks came to mean safety and I clung to that so eagerly that I began to fret about losing the trail. The contrast was gradually fading as the cloud and snow overhead thickened but this only made me more determined. With effort and rapt concentration I could still pick out the tracks as a single straight hairline of wan blue-ish light. I knew it was only a matter of time before the light would flatten completely so I rushed onward in a fit of irrational resolve. Once or twice I lost sight of the trail but forged on into limited visibility regardless, hardly daring to breathe as my gaze desperately swept the ground ahead for any sign. I was overwhelmed with gratitude each time I regained sight of the treasured blue hairline – only to be filled once again with the terrible desperation that comes with an expectation of loss.

Then it happened. I lost the tracks.

Swinging around on my skis, squinting into the white that was as blank and as impenetrable as the blackness of night, I desperately searched for any hint of the precious trail. I unhooked my harness from the sledge so that I could make slow spirals outwards from my position, scrutinising the ground for clues. I retraced my own tracks, only visible by the pinpricks of blue light left where the pointed tips of my ski poles had pierced the snow – but soon lost those as well. Having exhausted all possibilities, defeat brought me to a halt. I felt angry tears clog my airways.

Turning, I saw my sledges had shrunk into the middle distance so that they looked no bigger than miniature toys discarded in the snow. It shocked me how far I had wandered from my lifeline of food, fuel and shelter and mentally cautioned myself to be more careful as I skied back to them to re-attach my harness. I felt relieved to be re-connected to the sledges but as I set off I noticed I was nervous. The tracks had become a mental safety line to cling to and without them I felt more exposed than ever before. If the weather had been better, knowing that I was close to the skull and crossbones on my map would have been more manageable but as it was, blinded by blowing snow and psychologically weary, it seemed like I was blundering blindly through a minefield in which each and every step might send me through an unseen fissure in the ice below. The sense of trepidation amplified until it became intolerable. Glancing at my watch I knew I was due to ski for another hour. Despite being acutely aware that I couldn't afford to lose a precious hour of ski time, I gave in to my heightened emotional state and camped.

I pitched the Hilleberg sheepishly, knowing that I had capitulated to a foolishly exaggerated fear, and yet I didn't feel enough regret to make me change my mind. Once inside the tent I was quickly cosy in spite of the blustering weather outside. Sat in down booties and thermals, cradling a mug of warm fortified coffee and warmed by the stove that was busily melting snow, I unzipped the door a little to peer out at the gloom. There was not a single break in the clouds to give me any hope that conditions would improve when I woke. The sun was silent, giving me no clue as to how long it would be gone. I couldn't shake the thought that tomorrow I would have to travel through this obscured landscape so close to the crevassed area marked on my map. I imagined breaking through an undetected snowbridge, of falling until I became wedged between cold hard walls of ice, my ribs crushed by the impact, restricting my breathing. I visualised being suspended on a ledge, in the dark, cold and injured, desperately searching for a signal on my satellite phone, dialling numbers over and over in vain hope of connection. I pictured it all so well that it took on the definition of certainty. My imaginings started to feel like premonitions and I began to weep.

I knew that the tracks had offered little real security but in my desperation and exhaustion their loss appeared as a calamity of the most dramatic proportions. I came to the conclusion that there was no option but to find them. I put down my coffee, planting the mug securely in the snow, pulled my thin outer shell jacket over my thermals and stepped out of the tent. Without any distinct plan I paced across the snow, head bowed, eyes focused on the tight circle of snow around my feet where the reflection of colour from my blue down booties gave just enough contrast to be able to see the texture of the snow. Several times I spotted a slight feature and followed it eagerly only to find that it was a natural ridge of wind erosion or a change in the surface. I paced back and forth, turning back on myself and setting out again, chasing phantom tracks that turned out to be nothing but sastrugi and drift. With my eyes fixed on the ground I lifted my hood to protect my face from the blowing snow that was already collecting in my hair and eyebrows.

I don't know how long I scoured the blank whiteness but it was long enough for the hope and optimism that had been so strong on leaving the tent to fade into objectivity. I stopped and stared into the whiteout for a while, allowing myself to sob pathetically. I let the emotion flow out of me without check and without any analysis of what it was exactly that was causing the tears. I could think of a million causes at once: the effort, the exhaustion, the discomfort, the fear, the prospect of failure, the disappointment in my own lack of stoicism, the thought of all the days and miles to come, and, more than anything else, the ever-present, all-consuming alone-ness. Looking down at my feet in pitiful misery I noticed that through the thin soles of my down booties, my sole had left a near-perfect imprint in the snow, from my heel and the curve of my arch to each of my five toes. From my tracks it would appear I had been out in the snow in bare feet.

The sight snapped me back to my senses. I turned to see that my tent was nothing more than a dark smudge in the distance. With sudden clarity I became aware of my own dangerous stupidity. I was running around a potentially crevassed area of Antarctica, completely alone, inadequately dressed in thermals and a light windproof shell. I'd had the sense to grab both my GPS and satellite phone before leaving the tent but if I fell into a crevasse at that moment it is likely that neither would do me much good. If the fall didn't kill me and if, as was likely, I couldn't get a signal on my phone from within a fissure, it would be hours before I missed my first scheduled call to Union Glacier. Only then would anyone start looking for me. The chances of managing to keep myself alive for all that time in an excruciatingly cold crevasse without full clothing or even a hat were minimal.

More alarming than that, I remembered that I had stepped out of the tent without turning off my stove. I had been wandering around in the snow while, inside my precious and highly flammable Hilleberg, I had left a pan of melting snow simmering on an open flame. It would only take a gust of wind to nudge the tent fabric too close to the stove and it would take mere seconds for my tent and everything inside it to be consumed by fire. I would be left alone, without shelter and without clothing in an Antarctic whiteout.

I don't think I have ever done anything quite so stupid in my entire life.

I raced back to the Hilleberg tense with alarm, expecting it to combust in front of my eyes at any second. Reaching the door I checked and adjusted the stove before sitting in the porch gasping for breath, transfixed by my spectacular lack of judgement. Was this the decline in my reasoning that I had so feared? Had fear and panic, left unchecked by the absence of a team, driven me to reckless lunacy? Could I no longer rely on my own mind? I dissolved into despondent tears. I don't remember ever feeling so desperate. My scrambled thoughts couldn't seem to find one single positive to cling to. Above all I felt like a fool for putting myself into this situation. All my justifications for making this journey now seemed pathetically hollow. I would have given my soul in that moment for some solid semblance of safety, to be surrounded by friends, to have the security of a team, to be able to see a sound way home, to not have to run the gauntlet of crevasses for a single step more.

'Think…' I scribbled impatiently in my small notebook but I couldn't seem to find a shred of comfort in anything. My sense had deserted me.

I dreaded the morning and the mental anguish I knew it would bring. I expected the war of wills in my mind to be worse than ever.

I woke feeling overwhelmed with fear and desolation. Lying motionless in my sleeping bag, I recited under my breath the words above the tent door, now so worn as to be barely visible, 'Let routine take command of feeling.' I forced myself to think only of my jobs, to recall all the usual mind tricks to pull myself together, from imaginary team-mates to the most vicious of critics – only to dissolve into bleakness. I couldn't rid myself of the vision of lurking crevasses and the potential consequences should I find one. The fear was paralysing and no amount of careful logic could cut through it. I thought of the faith my family had in me not to get into trouble, of their belief that I would get myself home safely. The knowledge that I would let them down by venturing out of my tent when the risks felt so high only added to my misery.

I lingered over the remains of my coffee, listening to the wind. I knew it was the worst thing I could possibly do, that in allowing myself to imagine the feel of that wind, the sting of the cold, the empty hours of the ski, I was making the task ever harder. I knew this and yet I couldn't stop myself. I tried to understand the emotions I was wrestling with in the hope that being able to pinpoint the cause and rationalise them would reduce their potency. What is it about the sorrowful voice of the wind that cuts through all reason and logic to make us feel instinctively lonely and vulnerable? I searched my memories for any experiences that would make me associate the whine of the wind with fright or loneliness but found none; most of my storm memories involved being cosy and secure inside, safe from the weather. So was it conditioning by culture? Or is it something about the pitch and the form of the noise itself that unnerves us? Perhaps it is the fact that the mournful notes of the wind can sound almost human. Maybe it is not the noise itself but the constant movement causing it which brings loneliness to mind. We naturally associate movement with displacement, and displacement with sadness.

I noticed the shifting of air inside the tent pulling the steam from my coffee into ragged zigzags and then realised that it was in fact my hands shaking. Seeing the physical signs of my inner turmoil only heightened the fear.

'I'm not brave,' my mind wailed. 'I'm not courageous. I'm just Felicity and I can't do this.'

I had no special ability, no profound wisdom or technique that would help me get through this crisis of confidence. I had hit rock bottom and found there was no cerebral safety net. But through my desperation a horrid fact remained unchanged: there was no option but to find a way forward. I couldn't afford to wait for better weather. As deep as my despair might have been, my need was greater; if I wanted to reach the coast I had to get out of the tent. I thought about the last time I had decided not to move all those weeks ago. I remembered the disappointment on later realising that my reasons had been excuses, that it had been a self-deception borne by timidity. I wasn't going to let myself down like that again.

Still snivelling, and with my belly full of the nauseating static created by fear and anxiety, I struck camp and skied into the whiteout. I felt rigid with tension at first, expecting every slide forward to send me tumbling into a crevasse, but the mechanical rhythm of sliding one foot in front of the other relaxed me slightly and I drew confidence from the familiarity of the movement. When my friend the sun finally melted its way partially through the cloud cover, it lifted the light just a fraction. It was a subtle change but enough to enable me to see some faint contrast. It felt like a rescue and I noticed that I was breathing easier. Now I had greater hope of being able to spot any crevassing I came across. After several hours I began to veer cautiously west, creeping ever closer to the eighty-third line of latitude and into a landscape that I calculated to be safely beyond the scope of the crevassed area. As I crossed the line into the eighty-second degree, it felt like a death sentence had been lifted. I felt released from a choking vice of anxiety and I sensed that my celestial friend was as relieved as I was. Turning my face skyward, I couldn't see the sun except for a bright patch on the cloud-filled sky but I cried in gratitude anyway. Not only did I feel secure that the ground ahead was safer but I noticed too that the sky had changed from solid grey into a marbled quilt. Filtered sunlight played across the forward landscape like the lambency of candlelight, giving the terrain texture. The weather was breaking.

'Goodbye eighty-three,' I called out, taking a moment to glance at the murky horizon behind me and the ground that had caused so much upheaval.

Then I turned to the brighter view ahead and spoke a greeting from behind my face mask. 'Hello eighty-two.'

Watching the horizon sharpen I felt that same stab of combined wonder and despair that I had experienced so often in Antarctica. Frequently, when ploughing into a storm, battling with sastrugi or digging the Hilleberg out of drifts, there would be a part of my brain that registered I was cold and lonely and miserable – but there was another part of my brain rejoicing in the adventure of being in such a dramatic environment and relishing the discomforts. And so, when people ask me what was the worst and the best moment of my journey, I realise that often they were the very same thing and recall instants like these that were the worst and the best simultaneously.

Looking back on my expedition I can see that the most valuable lessons and insight resulted from experiences which, at the time, felt like the most miserable lows. I found that the clearest and most poignant recollections were those that had been the most challenging. These were the 'best' moments because I saw the 'best' of me in them. The last twenty-four hours had been among the most difficult of the entire journey but I would remember them as some of the most precious because I had been stripped to my lowest and still found a way to move on.

Like raking fallen leaves into heaps after a storm, I felt my brain drawing together my wits and patching over the crater left by the trauma of the morning. The coast was now only 200 nautical miles away which, if I continued at my current pace, could be as little as ten days of skiing. Ten days. It seemed so manageable and yet the reality was that each moment passed with such effort that ten days could have been a hundred years. Ten days was brief in the scheme of things but when I thought of repeating the day that had just passed ten times over, my confidence wavered.

The mental paranoia of the last two days had left me bruised. I was confused as to why I should be going through such emotional torment now, when I was so close to the end. But as I thought it over I realised that sensing the end was part of the problem. I had let my mental guard down and allowed my mind to rush ahead of my body. The disconnection was disastrous, just as it had been in the final kilometres before the Pole. I needed to refocus my attention on the present and revert to the guarded, clamped-down self that I had cultivated since my first day. I needed a mental reset, like pressing ctrl+alt+del on a computer to start again, and rebuild my defences. I had to be resilient against Antarctica and the alone-ness until the very end and not a moment sooner. There could be no short-cuts.

Sitting in the tent that evening I made a conscious effort to re-order my approach to the rest of the journey. I told myself that I was setting out on a ten-day expedition, starting the next morning. Sacrificing a whole blank page of my diminishing notebook I divided the remaining distance into ten daily mileage targets. Then I went through each bag of equipment in the tent, sorting, tidying and reorganising as I went. Finally I tackled my remaining rations. I amalgamated everything I had left into thirteen full bags to allow for ten days of skiing and three days of emergency overspill.

The result was a renewed sense of purpose. Starting out anew helped me to draw my mental focus back to the immediate future and it made me feel more centred, more steadfast, more determined.

Right from the outset I had been careful to limit my anticipation to the most pressing goal. On the Ross Ice Shelf I had thought only of the Leverett, on the plateau I had thought only of the Pole, leaving the Pole I had thought only of Thiels. At no point had I allowed myself to think of the whole; it was too big and too intimidating to think about all at once. Now, even though I was physically close to the end of my journey, I found that the 'end' was still too daunting to dwell on. My ability to process a goal had nothing to do with the number of miles or the number of days involved – instead it had everything to do with the importance I attached to the achievement of that goal. The end was so important that I couldn't process it yet. I had to focus on each step rather than the end result – and there were still plenty of steps to take.

It took me just three days to cover the eighty-second degree. Although I had been feeling ever fitter and stronger physically as I lost height from the Pole, I had skied a minimum of twenty nautical miles a day for the past twenty days without a break and I noticed the effects. Fatigue made my eyes feel gritty and my limbs heavy so that I frequently found myself hunched over my ski poles as I skied. In the evenings I skipped jobs so that I could get to sleep quicker and one evening I got dangerously close to falling asleep where I sat as I waited for snow to melt on the stove in the tent. The next morning I was so tired when I opened my eyes that I resolved immediately to give myself a day off. As I lay there, the plangent noise of the wind outside intruded on my dreams. I soon reduced the day off to a lie-in and finally, after half an hour of feeling uncomfortably guilty, I got up.

The weather had never completely cleared and today I marvelled at strange spikey clouds high in the atmosphere that crawled across the sky like white ivy. They were so spectacular that I skied as often as possible with my neck craned backwards to admire their unusual form and wondered what these odd clouds signified. A dark front had loomed on the horizon behind me all the previous day but I noticed that the sun had pushed it away from me to the west as it progressed so that it sat heavily on my left. I eyed the vaporous slick warily, trying to judge its movement as it lingered like a plume of pollution from distant industry.

When I saw them I was so surprised that I stumbled on my skis, crossing the tips in my astonishment and falling onto one knee in the snow. I ripped off my goggles to get a better look, stunned for a moment by the light. Then, sitting back on my heels with my skis beneath me, I cried through my laughter. Within the dark shadow of the weather front on my left were three nebulous lumps of denser colour. I realised that I had been able to see them for hours but hadn't recognised what they were. They were mountains and there was only one range of mountains they could possibly be. I was looking at the Ellsworths, the very same mountains I had sat contemplating all those weeks ago from Union Glacier, the range that marks the far coast of the continent. The dark triangular shadows in the distance might as well have been a big flashing neon sign in the sky announcing 'THE FINISH'. The end was – quite literally – in sight.

That day as I skied, each new horizon brought with it a new view and a new cluster of peaks until it seemed that the skyline was crowded with them. I was amazed at how quickly a shadowy lump transformed into a defined peak and at how quickly each cluster emerged out of the distance and became a part of the whole. I appeared to be skiing right into the arms of the mountain range and being surrounded by it. Three peaks in particular loomed proud of the rest and I eventually realised that this was because they were closer than the others. As their white rounded forms protruded ever larger I finally recognised them as the line of three pimple-like nunataks known as Three Sails. These were the peaklets I had seen from the plane on my way to the start of my journey.

I remembered how I had gazed down at them and had tried to imagine how I would feel when I saw those peaks again. Back then the expanse of Antarctica had been an unknown in my future. Now it was a memory in my past. In the time between I had gained exact knowledge of what crossing that expanse would entail. I now knew there would be endless days of whiteout, skies that could absorb the mind for weeks and moments of utter isolation. More importantly I knew how I would react to those challenges as a person. My ability to cope had perhaps been the biggest unknown of all and the greatest source of my pre-expedition nerves. I now knew that, despite tears and madness and anxiety, I would – and could – endure. I had been afraid to a greater or lesser extent every single day but looking back I understood that fear is not a weakness. It is how we deal with that fear that determines our strength. The knowledge that I was capable of persevering brought with it a gentle self-assurance. As a result, the person looking at the mountains having skied more than a thousand miles was a different woman to the one who had looked down on this exact spot some two months earlier.

I camped a few kilometres from the trailing peak of Three Sails and lingered in the brisk wind after pitching the tent to take in the skyline of summits that rose like stalagmites from the near horizon. It was clear why this place had been given the name 'Horseshoe Valley'. The mountains formed a broad amphitheatre with a narrowing neck. The next day I spent blissful hours skiing across the open ends of the horseshoe peering into the cul-de-sac of peaks in which every detail was razor sharp in the thin, supercooled air. Under the dazzling varnish of sunlight the rock faces shimmered iridescent gold or took on the paleness of ancient, weathered driftwood. It was a world the colour of foil and bone. Snow delicately frilled every ledge and filled every dip, layers of it compressed into ice under its own weight, glaciers bulging from hanging valleys like ripe fruit about to burst, the skin already cracked to reveal the almost fluorescent blues beneath. As the day progressed and the sun moved, the shades of the mountains deepened, the rock transformed from gold into the grey of an elephant's coarse cracked hide, while the snow morphed from brazen white into twilight blue.

Transfixed by the panorama on my left, I hadn't failed to notice the features appearing on my right. No more than a series of small black ovals on the horizon at first, several widely spaced nunataks rose reluctantly from the snowline. I suspected that the rock furthest to the east was Wilson Nunatak, the signpost I'd been told to look for to lead me to Hercules Inlet on the Ronne Ice Shelf. I pulled out my GPS to check. I wanted to be cautious because in the small area between my current position and Wilson Nunatak was perhaps one of the most notorious crevasse fields in Antarctica. Several expeditions a year cross this crevasse field, each following a carefully prescribed series of GPS coordinates distributed by ALE. The crevasses were well documented but knowing they were so close was unnerving.

Three years previously as I'd set out for the South Pole with my international team of women, another woman (a Major in the Canadian Air Force) had set out alone on a solo expedition to the South Pole from Hercules Inlet. A few days after leaving the coast she took off her skis and fell through the snowpack into an unseen fissure somewhere in this same crevasse field. Fortunately for her, she fell onto a ledge within the crevasse relatively near to the surface and was able to get a signal on her satellite phone. Not being far from her start point, ALE found her quickly and she'd been rescued having spent six long hours in the cold. (Considering how frightening the experience must have been, it is incredible that shortly after being rescued she restarted her expedition from the beginning. Crossing the crevasse field again, without incident this time, she went on to become the first Canadian to ski solo and unsupported to the South Pole.) The story had horrified me when I'd heard it, as all crevasse stories do, and it had stuck in my mind as I planned the route for this last part of my journey.

'Make sure you stick to the coordinates and you'll be fine,' Steve had reassured me at Union Glacier. 'And whatever you do, don't take off your skis.'

I followed his advice minutely, skiing carefully along precise coordinates using my GPS. When it was time to camp I took off just one ski at first and used it to thoroughly probe the ground around my camp site to check for any concealed fissures before pitching the tent.

It was perfectly still and brilliantly sunny. Pulling my sleeping bag from one of my sledges I deviated from my usual routine to lay it out on the snow in front of the Hilleberg and sat down to look at the mountains. According to my GPS I was less than ten nautical miles from Hercules Inlet where I would move from ice on land to the Ronne Ice Shelf that floated over the ocean, and complete my coast-to-coast traverse. It was entirely possible that the next day would be my last of the expedition. My attention was pulled into the view in front of me and lost in the space of it. The same oppressive silence that had filled my ears below the Transantarctic Mountains still throbbed at my temples now, but this time the silence didn't feel empty, it felt full of a noise created by the form and colour of the mountains. Even if the landscape wasn't full of life, it seemed to me now to be full of vitality. I wasn't alone, the landscape was packed with presence but I relished the simplicity of the solitude. Now that my alone-ness was coming to an end, I could enjoy the solitude and the isolation. I had Antarctica to myself and I liked it that way. I let my mind explore the prospect of seeing other people, of being back at Union Glacier surrounded by company and I became aware of my instincts shying away from the idea.

I had to laugh out loud at my own caprice, shaking my head in exasperation. I had struggled with the alone-ness for all this time and now here I was sentimentalising it. I reminded myself that little over a week before I had been dashing about blindly in an Antarctic whiteout looking for salvation in phantom tracks and scared out of my wits – literally. The solitude hadn't appeared so charming back then and I certainly hadn't relished the alone-ness in the despair of relentless bad weather.

The expedition had demonstrated forcefully that there is a difference between being by myself and true alone-ness. At home I regularly seek time to be on my own and find it a good way to sharpen my thoughts and focus my mind. It is a way of seeking respite from the onslaught of life that can occasionally become overwhelming and disorientating. I have spent days at a time hiking in the mountains there without seeing another human being – but this isn't true alone-ness. Even in the remotest regions of the UK it isn't difficult to spot the occasional glint of a rooftop and the vapour trails of aircraft during the day or the distant orange cast of a town's streetlights at night. Even if I hadn't seen or spoken to another human, the unmistakable existence of mankind had been plainly all around me. True alone-ness is something different. It is about losing the physical and mental safety net provided by human ties, about having no one but ourselves to rely on for safety or sanity. Humans are social animals, we are programmed through evolution to live within a tribe, and when we are beyond the reach of that tribe it goes against the deep grain of a prehistoric trait as fundamental as our senses or our need for children.

By being truly alone I had seen how deeply reliant I am on human ties and in ways that were unexpected. It was not simply a matter of having company to pass the time, or backup in case of an emergency. During the expedition, I found that the absence of others had shaped my behaviour, my thoughts, my actions, my reasoning. I had seen for myself that it is human relationships that bind us to place, time and purpose, human relationships that make us who we are as individuals and that our contentment, and our happiness, depend on those precious human connections.

CHAPTER NINE

GETTING OUT
OF THE TENT

@felicity_aston Another awesome day skiing past a parade
of beautiful mountains beneath crazy clouds. This last couple
of days have certainly been my reward.

@felicity_aston Just in case I was in danger of feeling
sentimental, a violent wind has appeared from nowhere and
is beating the tent like the bad old days.

As my route brought me closer to Wilson Nunatak I was seized
with the desire to climb to its summit. The idea was imprudent
in many ways; I was within striking distance of completing
a two-month, 1,700-kilometre journey that had stretched
me physically and mentally. The last thing I needed was any
extra exertion or an eleventh-hour injury. And yet, as the peak

revealed itself in ever greater detail, the more I was drawn to it. The nunatak was shaped like a blunted sphinx, its perfectly smooth contours rising into a low summit joined by a gentle saddle to a second, higher summit. My sight drifted up over its back and settled on the flattened hilltop at its crown. It looked like an uncomplicated hike and the summit promised an elevated 360 degree view, the exhilaration of being able to see forever, the inexplicable draw of being at the undisputed 'top' of something. As if in encouragement, the sun settled directly above the higher summit and surrounded itself with a spectacular halo like a presenting peacock. It was 22 January and the distance to the coast appeared in single figures on my GPS. For the first time on the expedition, I had time to spare.

At the base of the nunatak patches of snow and ice were stranded in the spaces between boulders, petering out by degrees higher up. I dragged my sledges onto one of the larger snow islands, securing them carefully with my skis so that there was no chance of them moving without me. The lower flanks of the nunatak were a jumble of fractured ledges and platforms of frost-shattered stone striped with distinct bands of coloured rock; some dark, some pale, some blotched with dabs of quartz. At first it felt strange to be on solid ground, to be stepping rather than sliding, but soon I was hopping from ledge to ledge, enjoying the sense of freedom. Without the weight of my sledges dragging behind me, I felt unnaturally buoyant. The gradient was easily manageable even in my square-toed ski boots and, contouring around the slope at a slight angle, I soon found myself on the lower of the two summits. Along the saddle, belts of light and dark rock formed concentric circles, one on top of the other. I stopped to look closer at the splinters of rock that littered the ground coloured in vibrant orange and ruddy brown that looked gaudy compared to the pastel shades I was used to. With another short climb I finally approached the higher summit of Wilson Nunatak. The wind greeted me, blowing hard from the open space ahead, and I stepped onto the lip of a dreamy skyscape of pearlescent cloud. Below, the glossy snow was streaked with ribbons of blue ice. Above it, surrounded by a delicate silver halo and gossamer cloud, blazed my friend the sun in triumphant approval. I nodded my grinning appreciation in its direction before turning my attention to the horizon on my left which was bristling with dark purple mountains, low and triangular, crowded together in a dense band. The extent of the Ellsworth Mountain range took me by surprise. My private panorama of mountains that had seemed so extensive as I crossed the narrow open neck of Horseshoe Valley had been, in reality, barely a glimpse of the range's toenail.

I sat on a boulder and breathed deeply in quiet satisfaction. The whole of Antarctica seemed to be mapped out below me. Shifting my position I turned my back to the wind and gazed southward at the horizon I had skied over. My mind led me back over the miles to where I had begun all those weeks before, and then continued back in time over the longer path that had brought me here. I thought about the anguish over the decision to walk away from conventional employment, of the endless search for ways to make expeditions happen and of creating a viable living around them. There had been no roadmap and yet looking backwards it all seemed so obvious, every step appearing to be part of an ordered sequence of events designed for the sole purpose of enabling me to be on this summit on this day.

It hadn't seemed so clear and ordered at the time. In hindsight, I had spent much of my twenties floundering in uncertainty and timidity, not being able to see a way forward and held back by the suspicion that I was making terrible mistakes. If only I could speak to myself back then and give reassurance that I was on the right track, that the decisions I was making would lead me to good places. But no one can tell you the way, you have to find it yourself – and the way is never clear until you step forward.

My thoughts turned to the less metaphorical 'way' that lay immediately ahead. I inspected the view to the north for any sign of the coast. It was difficult in the layers of shimmer to be sure what was cloud and what was snow but I thought I could see a deep cleft in the landscape close to the horizon, a richer shading that indicated an incline of some sort. Might this be Hercules Inlet? The thought gave me the momentum to move from my perch. I gave one last, longing look around at the view below me and turned to leave. It struck me then that I had climbed quickly to the top of the nunatak without pause and without feeling even the slightest bit out of breath. A climb like this, even when training for an expedition, would normally have left me gasping for air and my muscles burning. The constant low-intensity exertion of skiing and the extended time at higher altitudes must have left me in much better fitness than I appreciated. As I trotted down the same slopes back to my sledges I felt charged with energy and just a little bit pleased with myself. Reconnecting my harness to the sledges I felt unstoppable, all the fatigue of the past weeks forgotten and the coast within what felt to be no more than a short stride away. Little did I know that in the short distance that lay ahead to the very edge of Antarctica I would face some of the most demanding terrain of the entire journey.

The difficulty started almost immediately. The ground from the edge of the nunatak fell away into an immense windscoop with slicks of blue ice pooled at the bottom. There was no way to go around the windscoop completely as it tailed directly across my path but at least the slope down into it that lay directly ahead looked less severe than the gradients further to the left or right. There was nothing for it but to go straight down. I set off, holding my skis rigidly parallel to each other, feeling the glide of the slope beneath me. The crusted snow surface was studded with circular sastrugi that rose in platforms like inverted wedding cakes, the wind having eroded all the softer snow from around their bases, and they were as tough as plaster. As I picked up speed my ski tips were deflected from them like a pinball wizard. I was jolted off balance several times before finally pulling myself into a halt. My sledges, which had bounced violently along behind me, swung around on the rope attached to the harness at my waist and jack-knifed on the slope a few feet below, pulling me roughly forward. I paused for a moment, suspended precariously on the slope and rethought. I couldn't risk being pulled over and injured by my own sledges thundering down the slope behind me. Instead, I allowed my sledges to slide ahead like an eager dog taking its owner for a walk, and angled my skis against the slope so that I made steady but laborious zigzags down the glacis. It was awkward, so I was relieved when the slope began to flatten out. Eventually I felt confident enough to release the sledges, overtaking them as I glided downward under gravity. There was still enough of a gradient to pick up some speed. I squealed in delight as I clattered over the uneven sastrugi followed in hot pursuit by my sledges. Reaching the bottom panting but grinning I glanced upward at the slope we'd just descended. Disappointingly, from this angle it looked like the gentlest of inclines betraying nothing of what had caused the anxious restraint of the last few hours.

The ground ahead was flat but covered with the same mushroom-like sastrugi which made it feel like I was skiing over cobbles (even though I skied around the worst) and slowed my progress. Again and again I came down steep slopes, although none of them as dramatic as the incline beneath Wilson Nunatak. I stopped frequently to try and make sense of the scenery around me and match it to the view I'd had from the summit. It was clear that I was edging my way downwards, losing a lot of height and up ahead I could see a long line of dusky-blue shading protruding towards me from the east. It looked like a deep valley with a flat floor. I couldn't think of anything else this could be other than Hercules Inlet. Heading towards it, the sastrugi had been completely scoured away by the wind, revealing a solid surface of opaline ice which had been cratered into fist-sized dimples by the sun. Light glinted from every surface magnifying the glare so that as I approached the lip of the next slope it wasn't difficult to spot a ribbon of matt white snaking across my path. It was a snow-covered crevasse.

I cautiously approached the near side of the crack to get a better look. The snow that sagged slightly over the gap looked deceptively solid but I remained wary. It was a relatively narrow crevasse but still wider than the length of my skis and too wide for me to be confident of making a safe leap to the other side, even if I took off my skis. I allowed my eyes to follow its trail, a softly curving line that darted across the landscape for as far as I could see in either direction and looked unchanging right along its length. With little to recommend turning right or left,

I dithered for an instant before turning right (which at least looked slightly downhill). I skied along the edge of the crevasse for a little over a mile, stopping to inspect, then reject, several potential crossing places along the way. Finally the crevasse narrowed just enough for me to be able to place a tentative ski across the gap. My ski tip sat comfortably on the far edge while the back of my ski still rested securely on the near edge. I jabbed the ice on the other side hard with my ski pole to check that it felt as solid as it looked. Feeling confident I brought my other ski across so that my feet were suspended in parallel across the gap. Pausing like that for a moment I couldn't resist but plunge my ski pole into the snow bridge next to me, just to see what was beneath. The round basket at the end of my ski pole broke easily through the powdery snow and a chunk of the surface fell away like dust. Through the hole I could see the peculiar luminescent blue of light filtered through ice, and a glimpse of a terrifying blackness of a deep void. The glimpse was enough to make me step hastily onto the solid safety of the other side and drag my sledges quickly after me.

Glancing again at the hole I'd made with my ski pole I considered how lucky I was to have come across this crack in fine weather and clear sunshine in which every surface feature was as defined as an engineer's draft. The thought of what might have happened had I skied over this crevasse unknowingly in bad weather and flat light made my heart thump faster. I shuddered as if to shake off the thought and turned to look at the way ahead with renewed concentration. If there was one crevasse it was likely there would be more. Sure enough I crossed not one but two crevasses of a similar size, each time skiing along their edge until I found a safe place to cross. I felt confident but my anxiety increased as the hard icy surfaces ahead became covered by snowpack and low sastrugi. The snow would conceal any further crevassing in the ice beneath.

The planes being sent to collect me wouldn't be able to land on a slope; I had to reach flatter ground so I continued down slope after slope but I felt taut with nerves, worried that each step might send me plunging into a dark void. I ached to pitch camp, to be able to stay put and be safe rather than bear the excruciating suspense of what each stride might bring – but I couldn't stop where I was.

'Almost,' I told myself, noticing that my teeth were clamped tightly together in angst, my jaw taking the brunt of the nervous stress I felt.

The gradient ended abruptly on a narrow but flat plain surrounded on three sides by steep escarpments. This, I realised in amazement, was Hercules Inlet. The snow surface I stood on was ice floating on water (which is why it was so flat), a slim tongue extending from the main Ronne Ice Shelf to the east, whereas the surrounding escarpments were snow-covered shoreline. I could see a crease of colour in the snow at the base of the escarpments – as clear a sign of the coast as I was going to get in Antarctica – and by skiing across it I had completed my traverse.

I had arrived.

The numbers on my GPS confirmed that I was significantly north of the eightieth line of latitude which traced the coast and had therefore moved beyond the edge of the continent – but still I kept skiing. I headed onwards towards the centre of the inlet, feeling that I needed to reach something that was a definitive endpoint, but there was no clear finish line, no camp, no people, no silver globe to touch as a finishing post. I spied the low profile of an island in the middle of the inlet, pear-shaped with a large flat area on top, and, in the absence of anything better, I headed for that. As I approached the centre of the island I slowed my pace, dragging each ski steadily and deliberately to elongate every stride, until finally I stopped.

I squinted up at the sun.

'It's over,' I said aloud, partly to the sun and partly to myself. The sun was abnormally quiet for once, presumably as overcome by the surprise of the moment as I was. After counting the hours and the miles for so long it now all seemed to have come to an end too quickly. I reached for my water bottle and sat on my sledge in silence, gulping and watching the mountains. Having skied 1,744 kilometres in the previous fifty-nine days, I was now the first and only woman in the world ever to have crossed Antarctica alone.

I had traversed a continent.

I had skied across Antarctica.

The thought sounded absurd. It seemed barely credible to have skied so far, to have traversed an entire landmass, even though I could remember every stride, every moment, every inch. I imagined a map of Antarctica and my ski tracks leaving two unbroken parallel lines right the way across it. It was like looking down from the top of a ladder and realising for the first time how high I had climbed. While climbing you have to focus on each rung, absorbed by each new footing and only when safely at the top can you appreciate the view. Similarly, I had needed to be absorbed by each footfall, by the individual incidences of each day and only now could I start to see how far those footfalls had carried me. It was hard to take in. Just as the scale of the journey had prevented me thinking of the whole, now it prevented me from being able to appreciate what had been completed. I didn't feel triumphant and I wasn't filled with a sense of achievement; there was just surprise and perhaps a small sense of anti-climax. After all, I was still alone, just me and Antarctica, exactly as it had been for the past two months.

I pulled out my satellite phone and sat with it in my lap for a moment before calling Union Glacier. Beneath the congratulations, I could hear relief in Steve's voice that I was done and sensed that I was now one less concern in a hugely complex logistical picture he was wrestling with as the season drew to a close. They were going to send a plane for me within hours.

'I promise you that by this evening you'll be in the warm with a glass of red wine,' Steve told me.

As I rang off the thought of the promised comfort and imminent company broke through my sense of bewilderment and, at last, the tears came.

I was going home.

The alone-ness that had pressed down on me for so long and held me in taut high-alert would soon be replaced with the warmth and security of company. Within hours I would be able to release myself from mental hibernation and relax into a more familiar version of myself. All I had to do was sit tight.

I woke to cheerful sunlight filtering through the bright yellow lining of my faithful Hilleberg and felt rigidly tense. Then I remembered. Today I didn't have to leap out of my sleeping bag to chase the horizon – I was already where I had to be. I relaxed into the warmth and let my mind settle. The previous evening I'd set up my tent to wait for the plane and called Union Glacier on the hour every hour to report on the weather for the pilots – but each time I did so I was told that the plane had been delayed a little longer. Eventually Steve came back on the phone. Mindful of his promise of red wine by the end of the night, he was apologetic.

'I'm so sorry, Felicity, but the weather has deteriorated this end so we won't be able to come and get you tonight.'

The weather had played one last trick on me but I wasn't sorry. I needed a last evening alone with Antarctica. It felt appropriate. I needed time to digest the fact that my journey was over and to prepare myself for company again.

That morning I took my time making breakfast coffee from my meagre remaining rations while still nested in the comfort of my sleeping bag. I was aware of a deep relief unfolding and a steadfast sense of satisfaction spreading into every corner of my being but, through my contentment, an insistent thought rose adamantly to the surface. It was very similar to a thought that had occurred to me three years before when standing alone at the South Pole for the first time. The thought was the knowledge that on that morning, as on every morning for the last two months, I could have got on my skis and headed across the snow. Tired as I was I knew that my muscles were capable of another day. My mind imagined packing up and skiing away, which led quickly to the inevitable next question; if I was sure I could continue, how far would I be able to ski?

I tried to gauge what capability I had left in me both physically and mentally. Would I realistically be able to ski all day? Did I feel strong enough to ski for another week? Would it be conceivable to turn around and ski another 2,000 kilometres back to where I had started?

I expressed a silent, inward groan. These are the questions, this is the curiosity, that has led me back to the polar regions again and again. Within hours of finishing the most ambitious expedition of my life I was already being drawn on to think of new challenges and my heart sank a little with the weight of it. I could see how easily the bid to find extremes of capability could transform from a mode of motivation into a source of torment. Filling the hole left by an expedition with the seeds of a new adventure was a temptation I was wary of, knowing as I did both its compelling addiction and the fact that it has no end. But I couldn't avoid the question circling my brain. If I had succeeded in crossing Antarctica alone, did it mean that I was capable of more? After all, it is only when we have tried our best and failed that we know we have reached our absolute potential. Was what I had been searching for all this time not success but, in fact, failure?

I shook the thoughts from my head. I had come to Antarctica to explore my limits but I realised now that I had arrived with a preconception of what that limit would look like. I had envisaged falling to my knees in the snow with the conviction that I couldn't go on. I imagined that I would be able to describe my limit in terms of a number of miles and a number of days. I had been wrong. The last two months had taught me that a personal limit is not as defined as a line in the snow. No matter how far we travel or how hard we push, our bodies will keep moving forward and our minds will find ways to process. But in exploring those extremes we pay a price. I may have covered every mile in Antarctica from coast to coast but there had been mornings on the ice when I had felt in real danger of losing my mind, times when I had felt more desperate and desolate than at any other time in my life and I never wanted to experience that kind of despair again. There is a price I'm not willing to pay in order to discover the absolute extent of my personal limits. I have pushed far enough. Through the prism of Antarctica I had found my answer, I had found my limit. My limit was being alone.

By mid-afternoon I began to worry that I would need to eke my rations out over another night when I received word from Union Glacier that the plane was on its way and would be with me within the hour. I packed away all my belongings, leaving just the shell of my tent as a precautionary shelter, and stepped outside to wait. A constant breeze streamed past me from the north but the sun glared in heatless intensity through a loose patchwork of high cloud. Expectation raced through me as both excitement and panic; excitement that I was going home but panic at the thought of my expedition being over. I had longed for the plane to return ever since it had left me – but I had also dreaded it. Since leaving the Pole I had feared its appearance because it would mean I had run out of time. Now, I dreaded it because the plane heralded the passing of something that I would never experience again. My big adventure was over and, as demanding as it had been, there was a sadness in the finality of going home.

I pulled out my camera and started to take pictures. I took pictures of the horizon, of the tent, of myself. It wasn't as if I didn't already have a million images of almost precisely identical scenery but I think I knew even then that I wasn't taking pictures to capture the view. It was an instinctive act to try and capture something of the moment – as if the pixels of my camera could trap not just light but a sense of the experience too.

I heard it before I could see it. A faint drone barely perceptible above the fizz of silence. Scanning the horizon to the west I spotted the plane while it was still no more than a microscopic dot low over the mountains. It grew and expanded until I could see the dark slash of its wings and the distinctive silhouette of a Twin Otter. It brought back memories of standing beneath a different range of mountains on the opposite side of the continent and once again I couldn't quite untangle how it was possible that I'd skied across an entire landmass. I didn't have any special abilities, I wasn't superhuman and yet here I was on the far coast of Antarctica. It was clear to me that the success of my expedition had not depended on physical strength or dramatic acts of bravery but on the fact that at least some progress – however small – had been made every single day. It had not been about glorious heroism but the humblest of qualities, a quality that perhaps we all too often fail to appreciate for its worth – that of perseverance. Critical to skiing across Antarctica had been the distinctly unimpressive and yet, for me, incredibly demanding challenge of finding the will to get out of the tent each and every morning. If I had failed in that most fundamental of tasks, then my expedition would have been over.

The plane landed in a flash of glinting metal and a roar of thrumming engines. I sheltered my eyes from the sun to watch as it dragged a nebulous cloud of ice vapour around itself, before turning and trundling back towards me. As I watched, I made an internal pact with myself to remember that it is as vital to celebrate daily successes – even those as marginal as getting out of the tent – as it is to analyse failures; that one small success every day will eventually add up to a greater achievement; that looking back to fully appreciate how far we have come is as essential as looking forward to where we want to be.

The shadow of the plane's wing fell on the snow around me and the rush of backdraft from the engine lifted spindrift into the air. I stepped forward to dismantle my home on the ice for the very last time. While I rolled tent material and plucked anchors from the snow in a series of movements made slick and rapid by repetition over the last sixty days I sensed the impression of something important crystallising in my subconscious. The fact that I had crossed Antarctica, despite the tears and the fear and the alone-ness, deepened my belief that we are each far more capable than we give ourselves credit for. Our bodies are stronger and our minds more resilient than we could ever imagine. To entrench it in my brain and carry it with me out of Antarctica, I summarised this important realisation in one simple phrase:

Keep getting out of the tent.

If I can do that, each and every day, no matter the challenge, who knows where the next day will take me.

EPILOGUE

ECHOES AND SHADES

@felicity_aston Having to remind myself of the rules now I'm not alone; no peeing where I stand, no talking to the sun, no snot or dribble on my face...

@felicity_aston The mug I've been happily using (but not washing) for the last two months now looks like a biohazard to me – clear sign I am readjusting.

@felicity_aston My non–expedition clothes are revealing just how much I've changed – feels like I've found someone twice my size and stolen their jeans.

I used to have a camera that was metallic, heavy and completely mechanical with two solid lenses that fastened onto its clunking body. The lenses shared a circular polarising filter that fitted onto the end of whichever lens I was using. The filter split the light so that as it was rotated the quality of the colours seen through the camera altered. When the filter was perfectly aligned the colours snapped into an intense brilliance that made what had been before seem dampened and clouded. Although the scene through the viewfinder hadn't changed, the filter made it appear clearer, richer and more tangible. Returning from my journey across Antarctica I felt that my experience had a similar effect, lending the simple details of life an extra bloom and defining understandings that had been hazy before. My perspective had shifted in barely perceptible but significant ways that it took me time to notice and identify.

During the first months at home the only difference I was aware of was a slight disconnection between my surroundings and my inner landscape. My brain seemed to be somewhere else and I often found that it had wandered back to Antarctica. Getting on a train one morning from my seaside home I sat looking out of the window and saw a flat white horizon above a landscape calloused by sastrugi. I blinked in confusion and a second later realised that it wasn't sastrugi – it was the ocean roughened by low, choppy waves and bleached by the pale reflection of an overcast sky.

These mental mirages faded in time and I recognised more fundamental differences. I was filled with new certainty and detected a placid but resolute composure in myself that was unfamiliar. It was a confidence that came from having persevered, mixed with the relief of being released from a long-standing unknown – that of my own capability. I returned with a better perception of what was important to me as a person and with more understanding of the factors that drive my decisions and motivations. I still feel the pull of adventure but I have a clearer idea of the challenges that will be meaningful to me in the future. None of this insight would have been possible had I not been on my own. I was glad for the experience of isolation and I know I will continue to benefit from the memories of the solitude in Antarctica (both good and bad), but I also know that being alone for so long and in such a place is not something I will ever want to repeat.

Not that there weren't aspects of life on the ice that I missed. Having learnt to live without thought, I was surprisingly reluctant to let all the thinking back in again. In Antarctica I had been driven by the momentum of routine and it took a while on my return to get used to the mental white noise of normal life. Pleased as I was to be home (my first hot shower was lengthy and was quickly followed by a second – just because I could), I regularly found myself longing for the compact security of my yellow-and-green Hilleberg. The tent that had felt like a tomb during the first days of the expedition had come to be a sanctuary towards the end, a place of comforting safety. In the tent my few essentials were arranged conveniently within arm's reach, made simple by the lack of surplus. I found that, at home, I missed that simplicity and convenience. Going about my life it seemed that whatever I needed was obscured by the choice of options and that nothing I needed was ever where it was supposed to be – it always involved a journey, be it to another room or to the shops or to another town. It is interesting how quickly I'd got used to living with just the basics and how long it took me to adjust to having more.

I hesitate to admit it, but there was another legacy of my time alone. In the weeks and months that followed the expedition what I felt most keenly of all was the absence of a companionship that had become central to my experience of solitude in Antarctica. I first became aware of it within days of arriving home. Sitting by a window in a London hotel, I felt a warm swathe of sunlight fall on my arm. The touch of the light was as real as a tap on the shoulder. It was a demand for my attention. I looked up to follow the light and saw that the sun had broken dramatically through the cloud outside. Like me, the sun was stronger now, unimpeded by the demands of the Antarctic but still recognisable as the same character that had travelled with me for all those miles. I smiled in genuine pleasure to see my friend and lifted my arm to wave, opening my mouth to say hello.

I stopped myself just in time. Turning abruptly to the others in the room I paused, embarrassed, waiting to see if anyone had noticed my slip. My instinctive reaction had been to greet the sun as I had done for so many days, but a lifetime of social training arrested the urge (thankfully). This was not behaviour I wanted others to witness. Talking to the sun was not something I could do in company.

The sun beamed on, reaching out to me as it used to do but I studiously ignored it. Instantly I was gripped with an acute sense of guilt. This was the companion who had seen me through the desperate days, who had fought through blizzard and storm to provide the companionship I had so badly needed and yet, now that I was safely at home and had no need for its consolation, I was abandoning my faithful friend. My failure to acknowledge its importance and loyalty felt despicable. As I wrestled with my guilt I hoped that the sun would understand my predicament, that it would sense my genuine gratitude and see why I couldn't acknowledge its support in public – but I had come to know the sun well enough to suspect that, in fact, it would be furious with me. I worried that, should I ever need the companionship of the sun again, my jilted friend would refuse to come to my aid.

And so, even now, more than a year after returning from the Antarctic, you might catch me looking upward on a sunny day – and when no one is watching I still give the sun a nod and a wave. I lift my face to the light, beaming mental greetings, and the sun seems to respond by blazing back at me just a little brighter.

AUTHOR'S NOTE

When Eugene Kaspersky met my parents his first words were an apology. He had assumed they would be livid at him for providing the funding that enabled me to ski alone across Antarctica. It was another example of the ways in which Kaspersky Lab is a wonderfully unconventional and welcoming sponsor and I feel very fortunate to have earned the support of Eugene, Randy Drawas and many others who have been instrumental in the partnership. It is clear that they genuinely care.

I am grateful for equal care and enthusiasm from the indomitable Stephanie Solomonides who looked after my life for me while I was on the ice and who has more than once expertly handled a distraught polar explorer sobbing on the line.

Meriting the belief of others is endlessly humbling and inspiring. Henry and Melodie Yates were among the first to back my big ambition and I will always remember their generosity and faith. Similarly I am indebted to Wendy, Alan and Susan Grummit of CGR Group (not least for Polar Koala).

The Transglobe Expedition Trust not only allocated funding to my journey but also later presented me with the Ginny Fiennes Award, of which I am tremendously proud.

I benefited from infinite encouragement from many quarters including Chestfield Rotary Club, staff and students at Hartsdown Technology College, Brian and Julie Powell, Sue Sutherland of Scott Bailey LLP and Sir Roger Gale MP. I'd particularly like to thank staff and students at Birchington Primary School who were so upset to hear that Father Christmas might not visit my tent on the Antarctic Plateau on 24 December that they bought me a special present to take with me (the jelly babies were much appreciated!) and later adopted a polar bear which they named 'Felicity' in my honour.

I am indebted to many people who went out of their way to help me prepare for the expedition. Massive thanks to Steve Jones at Antarctic Logistics and Expeditions for continuing to give dependable advice (and I forgive you for the pre-emptive promise of red wine), Dr Stephen Pack of the School of Sport and Exercise Science at the University of Hertfordshire, Gísli Jónsson at Arctic Trucks (your pivot design for the sledges was flawless as expected), Dr Ross, Valdi Gudmundsson, and Andrew Moon.

Sponsorship is precious and I never take for granted the wonderful relationships that have developed with some great companies over the years. I'd particularly like to thank Richard Woodall at Mountain Equipment, Jo Allen and Paul Cosgrove at Montane, Tony and Alison Simmonds at Fuizion Freeze-Dried Foods, Hans Falkenburg and Alison Upton at Cotswold Outdoor (as well as Elaine Boswell and colleagues at Cotswold Outdoor Maidstone), Petra Hilleberg at Hilleberg The Tentmaker, Nick Farrell at Yellowbrick Tracking, Jeff

White at Iridium, Harvey Hipperson, Tracey Harris and Charlotte Thornton at AST-UK, Lauren Heape at Biocare, James O'Malley and Giles Bryan at Ipadio, Colin Pickering at Bloc Eyewear and the wonderful Soren Braes. I also greatly appreciate support from Fantasea, Cold Avenger, Anglo-Dal (for the all-important Sesame Snaps), Pol Roger and High Five.

In Punta Arenas the wait for good weather was transformed by the good company of both Ruth Storm and Olga Mallo (I hope to share many more Pisco Sours with each of you in the future). I am also thankful to Gunni and Saeunn for presenting me with knock-out Icelandic pharmaceuticals that saved the day in Punta and to Alejandro and family at Hostal La Estancia who not only welcomed me as a semi-permanent house-guest but also gave me the best breakfast of my life on my return from Antarctica (cooked eggs, hot buttered bread rolls and fresh chilled strawberries with grapes).

For inspiration and sanity I owe a lot to Paul Deegan, the new Mrs Bloomfield, Sarah Outen, Nancy Moundalexis (for the cookies and note) and to the five faces that felt like a miracle when they appeared on the plateau; Gísli, Gummi (not forgetting your industrious grandmother), Steve, Tony and Jim. Music was important to me while skiing and although they may never know that they helped to propel a woman across Antarctica, I am indebted to Junip, Other Lives, Low, Gus Gus, Caribou, Florence + the Machine, Turin Brakes, Ben Howard, Beth Orton, Elbow and Lamb amongst others. I would also like to especially thank everyone who followed me on Facebook and Twitter, particularly those who introduced themselves to the 'Twittersphere' specifically for the purpose – your enthusiasm had real impact – and especially Don Pietro Damian for sharing his thoughts. Additional thanks to the many ex-FIDS who got in touch after the expedition. It meant a lot to have the support of fellow winterers and Marguerite Bay-ers, including the British Antarctic Monument Trust for which I am pleased to be an ambassador.

I have many reasons to thank my family but what principally springs to mind in this case is the huge box of doughnuts you brought with you to the airport for me to devour on the way home (how well you know me!). But I also need to thank Dad for the history, Auntie Wendy for the St Christopher that kept me safe and to my sister, Alex, for the locket. It will forever be one of my most treasured possessions.

I first heard Joanna Lumley speaking about her time alone on a castaway island at the Royal Geographical Society a few months after my return from Antarctica. I was enthralled by a sense of wonder in her words that reminded me of my own response to solitude and so I am thrilled to bits that she agreed to write the foreword for this book. Joanna – Thank you.

I also owe thanks to my other personal heroes: Ann Bancroft and Liv Arnesen, who kindly gave permission for me to quote them from their book, *No Horizon Is So Far* (Penguin Books, 2004); and Erling Kagge for allowing me to quote from the wonderful, *Philosophy For Polar Explorers* (Pushkin Press, 2006).

It was far harder to write about the expedition than I ever supposed and I must thank both Jennifer Barclay and Abbie Headon for believing in the potential of the results (and for being so understanding with deadlines) but I must also thank everyone who bought my first book, *Call of the White: Taking the World to the South Pole*, especially those who contacted me afterwards. Knowing that it meant something to you is a source of motivation for me to write more and to write better.

Finally, I would like to dedicate this book to anyone who has ever struggled to 'get out of the tent'. Whatever the form and type of your personal challenge, remember that the days pass, the mind copes and we emerge as better, stronger people. You are infinitely braver and more resilient than you imagine.

ABOUT THE AUTHOR

Trained as a physicist and meteorologist, Felicity's first polar experience was as a scientist with the British Antarctic Survey, where she spent three years living on the continent monitoring climate and ozone.

In 2009, Felicity led the largest and most international women's team ever to make the 900-kilometre ski journey to the South Pole. This record-breaking expedition involved members from across the Commonwealth, many of whom had never even seen snow before. The expedition took thirty-eight days, arriving at the Pole in time to celebrate the sixtieth anniversary of the Commonwealth. Felicity told the story of this adventure in her book *Call of the White*, published by Summersdale in 2011.

Previous notable expeditions include the first British women's crossing of Greenland, a 700-kilometre winter crossing of Lake Baikal in Siberia and an adventurous expedition in Iceland for young people with a brain injury. She was also part of the first ever all-female team to complete the Polar Challenge, a 360 mile endurance race to the Magnetic North Pole.

CALL OF THE
WHITE

TAKING THE WORLD TO THE SOUTH POLE

EIGHT WOMEN
ONE UNIQUE EXPEDITION

'enthralling'
WOMAN'S WEEKLY

FELICITY ASTON

CALL OF THE WHITE

Taking the World to the South Pole

Felicity Aston

ISBN: 978-1-84953-134-4   Paperback   £9.99

Could YOU ski to the South Pole?

That was the challenge that British adventurer Felicity Aston put to women from around the Commonwealth, as she set out to create the most international all-female expedition ever to the Pole. The team would not be experienced explorers but 'ordinary' women who wanted to inspire others to follow their dreams or make a change for the better in their lives. She received more than 800 applications. 'What is skiing?' asked someone in Ghana.

At the close of 2009, Felicity led a team from places as diverse as Jamaica, India, Singapore and Cyprus – some of whom had never even seen snow or spent the night in a tent before joining the expedition – on one of the toughest journeys on the planet.

'An uplifting and enthralling feat; I take my fur hat off to all those who answered this call of the white. An inspiring tale which will stir the hearts of women and men around the world'   Benedict Allen

'True inspiration to venture beyond your comfort zone'
                                                    Wanderlust magazine

Have you enjoyed this book?
If so, why not write a review on your favourite website?

If you're interested in finding out more about our books, find
us on Facebook at **Summersdale Publishers** and follow us on
Twitter at **@Summersdale**.

Thanks very much for buying this Summersdale book.

www.summersdale.com